Understanding the F-Word

Understanding the F-Word

F-Word

American Fascism and the
Politics of Illusion

David McGowan

Writers Club Press
San Jose   New York   Lincoln   Shanghai

Understanding the F-Word
American Fascism and the Politics of Illusion

Writers Club Press
an imprint of iUniverse.com, Inc.

For information address:
iUniverse.com, Inc.
5220 S 16th, Ste. 200
Lincoln, NE 68512
www.iuniverse.com

ISBN: 0-595-18640-8

Printed in the United States of America

For my parents, siblings, progeny, and various other members of the McGowan and Griffith families. And, as always, for Gretchen.

Epigraph

And it seems to me perfectly in the cards that there will be within the next generation or so a pharmacological method of making people love their servitude, and producing...a kind of painless concentration camp for entire societies, so that people will in fact have their liberties taken away from them but will rather enjoy it, because they will be distracted from any desire to rebel by propaganda, brainwashing, or brainwashing enhanced by pharmacological methods.

Aldous Huxley, 1959

Through clever and constant application of propaganda people can be made to see paradise as hell, and also the other way around, to consider the most wretched sort of life as paradise.

Adolf Hitler, 1935

Contents

PART I
Understanding the F-Word

Fascism denies that the majority, by the simple fact that it is a majority, can direct human society; it denies that numbers alone can govern by means of a periodic consultation, and it affirms the immutable, beneficial, and fruitful inequality of mankind, which can never be permanently leveled through the mere operation of a mechanical process such as universal suffrage.

Benito Mussolini, 1932

Chapter 1

Who Are You Calling A Fascist?

We stand for the maintenance of private property ... We shall protect free enterprise as the most expedient, or rather the sole possible economic order.

Adolph Hitler

The current political system in place in the United States at the dawn of the twenty-first century is fascism. Of course, we don't like to call it that. We like to call it 'democracy.' Nonetheless, it looks an awful lot like fascism, though to understand how this is so requires an awareness of what fascism actually is.

It is a system that we, as a nation, have long had a fascination with. It has been the preferred means of governing in US-controlled 'Third World' satellites for decades. Of course, we don't call it fascism there either, whether in Southeast Asia, Latin America or elsewhere. We call it 'anti-communism' or even 'Western-style democracy,' but never the f-word.

We don't like to use the f-word at all. It tends to conjure up unpleasant images. Our perceptions of fascism are shaped both by the very real horrors of the Holocaust, and by the fictional worlds created by writers with British and American intelligence connections like Aldous Huxley and George Orwell.[1] These are the images that our schools and our media provide for us.

So when we think of fascism, we think of concentration camps filled with corpses and horribly decimated walking skeletons. We think of a stiflingly regimented society in which 'Big Brother' watches our every move. We think of brutal pogroms by jack-booted thugs, and violent repression of dissenting views.

These images are so far removed from the world that we live in that we cannot conceive that our system of governance could have the remotest resemblance to that which was in place in Nazi Germany. The problem is that fascism, viewed from the inside through a veil of propaganda, rarely looks the same as it does when viewed from the outside with the benefit of historical hindsight.

To most of those living in Germany during the reign of the Third Reich, fascism didn't look the way that we think it is supposed to look either. To many, in fact, it looked like a pretty damn good system (of course, Jews living in the ghettos of Warsaw had a much different view of German fascism, just as African Americans living in America's 'inner cities' have a much different view of American fascism).

That is why, at the end of the war—when the whole world looked in horror at the German people and asked how this could

---

[1] As documented in Martin Lee and Bruce Shlain's *Acid Dreams* (Grove Press, 1985), Huxley had extensive connections to the CIA, particularly to psychiatrists on the agency's payroll involved in MK-ULTRA research. Orwell, who studied under Huxley at Huxley's alma mater, Eton, went to Burma afterwards to serve as an officer in the Indian Imperial Police, an appendage of British military intelligence. Orwell later received extensive funding by the CIA ("The Intelligentsia and the CIA," *The Independent*, June 28, 1999).

be—they replied that they "just didn't know." And though many denied knowledge of Nazi brutality to avoid prosecution for war crimes, there were undoubtedly a good many people who could honestly claim that they *didn't* know. Nevertheless, a world shocked and repulsed by the extreme depravity of a fascist state run amok would not accept as an answer that "we just didn't know."

This answer was unacceptable because there was no way to reconcile the horrific images with the people's pleas of ignorance. We could not accept that a regime so fundamentally criminal and corrupt would not have revealed itself to its people as being so. We would not accept, and still will not, that the fascist state does not present to its people the face that we have been taught to recognize.

One mistake we make is in equating fascism with the Holocaust. The Holocaust represented one extreme manifestation of European fascism, but did not in-and-of itself define what fascism is, despite the fact that our education on the subject tends to encourage the belief that this was indeed the event that defined the Third Reich.

The indoctrinated belief that fascism is synonymous with the Holocaust deliberately confuses the issue of what exactly fascism is. So too does the highly stylized versions presented in works such as *1984* and *Brave New World*. These books, and others like them, have created an unrealistic consensus view of what the authoritarian state looks like, and by doing so have given us a false sense of security.

We think we know what fascism looks like and we therefore think we are safe from it. Never would we allow the Holocaust to take place on our shores, nor the creation of a regimented, controlled, dystopian society. But to truly protect ourselves from the evils of fascism, we need to look beyond our preconceived notions of what the f-word actually means.

We need to recognize that these extreme examples of police state excesses obscure our view of what fascism actually is, about who the system serves and about how and why it is maintained. We need to recognize that the face of fascism need not be the personification of evil.

The first step towards understanding what we are as a nation (though not as a people), and what we stand for, is to clearly define exactly what fascism is. To do so, I can think of no better authority to turn to than the *Webster's New World Dictionary*, apparently the self-proclaimed wordsmiths of the New World Order, which offers the following definition:

fascism: a system of government characterized by rigid one-party dictatorship, forcible suppression of opposition, private economic enterprise under centralized government control, belligerent nationalism, racism, and militarism, etc.

It should be readily apparent that some aspects of this definition, most notably the notion of private economic enterprise, bear an uncomfortable similarity to the American 'democratic' system. Luckily, though, the people at *Webster's* realize that changing times sometimes require changing definitions.

In truth, the definition above is not the current one offered by *Webster's*, but is taken from an ancient 1980 edition of the *New World Dictionary*, hardly relevant to today's modern world. A more recent variation, taken from the 1990 edition, shows that a not-so-subtle change has occurred in the definition of, if not the practice of, fascism:

fascism: a system of government characterized by dictatorship, belligerent nationalism and racism, militarism, etc.

Gone now is that whole unpleasantness about private economic enterprise that might have, perhaps, struck a little too close to home. So we can all sleep well knowing that even as the country creeps ever closer to overt fascism, *Webster's* will thoughtfully rewrite the dictionary so that we may maintain a comfortable distance between ourselves and the dreaded f-word..

Now some may argue that this tendency to rewrite the dictionary—to rewrite history if you will—is in-and-of itself indicative of fascism. While a perfectly reasonable argument, a much better case can be made that America is indeed a fascist state by comparing actual conditions in the US today with *Webster's* authoritative definition.

Chapter 2

Fascism Deconstructed

Fascism is a dictatorship from the extreme Right, or to put it a little more closely into our local idiom, a government which is run by a small group of large industrialists and financial lords ... I am going to ask latitude to insist that we might have Fascism even though we maintained the pretense of democratic machinery. The mere presence of a Supreme Court, a House of Representatives, a Senate and a President would not be sufficient protection against the utter centralization of power in the hands of a few men who might hold no office at all. Even in the case of Hitler, many shrewd observers feel that he is no more than a front man and that his power is derived from the large munitions and steel barons of Germany.

syndicated columnist Heywood Broun, 1936

To begin, we will need to break the definition down into its component parts. I should note here that we will be using the earlier—and more complete—definition, on the assumption that fascism, as a concept, hasn't really changed much in the past twenty years.

We begin then with the notion that—according to the good people at *Webster's*—fascism is a system of government characterized by:

1. rigid one-party dictatorship
2. forcible suppression of opposition

3. private economic enterprise under centralized government control
4. belligerent nationalism
5. racism
6. militarism

As the first two components are the most debatable and require the longest explanations, we shall skip these for now and move first to the more obvious manifestations of fascism currently on display in America, beginning with component number three – *private economic enterprise under centralized government control.*

This certainly sounds like an accurate capsule description of the US economic model, otherwise known as the Western democratic model, as it apparently did to the people at *Webster's*. It is, at any rate, an accurate description of how we, as loyal Americans, are supposed to *believe* that the system works.

In theory, at least, there is supposed to be centralized control over private enterprise, to enforce such concepts as fair labor standards, environmental protections, and anti-trust legislation. In truth, however, the heads of corporate America are also its heads of state, and are essentially regulating themselves. Or, more accurately, failing to do so.

But the point is that the way the system is *supposed* to work is for private enterprise to be under federal regulation. The federal government is supposed to rein in monopoly corporate power and guarantee that workers and the environment get a fair shake, in addition to setting monetary policy.

The way the fascist state actually works, however, is for the centralized government to be under the control of private economic enterprise. This is as true today in America as it was in fascist Italy and Germany. So this aspect of the definition is clearly applicable to the US political/economic system. We can then move on to the next component – *belligerent nationalism*.

When I think of belligerent nationalism, I think back to early 1991, a time when it was not possible to drive even a few blocks to the local video store without passing a stream of American flags and yellow ribbons flapping in the wind. A time when one couldn't turn on the television without seeing a mob of people in a field somewhere creating a giant human American flag.

I think of the pompous theme music and 'Desert Storm' miniseries style graphics on CNN, and the relentless braying of military and government hacks as they barely contained their exuberance while discussing 'sorties,' 'air supremacy,' and 'smart bombs.' I think of a nation so inflated with its own sense of self-importance and self-righteousness that it openly cheered each airing of sanitized video footage of bombing attacks on largely defenseless civilian targets.

And then I think that while America was busy patting itself on the back and beating its chest, the conditions were being created that would result in the deaths of as many as 2,000,000 Iraqis, over 60% of them children under the age of ten.[2]

That's over a million children, for anyone who's counting. And not one of them had anything to do with the planning or execution of the annexation of Kuwait. Nor were any of them involved in the building of any 'weapons of mass destruction,' or the oppression of the Kurdish people of Iraq. But they're all dead now

---

2   David McGowan *Derailing Democracy*, Common Courage Press, 2000, chapter 27. Note: this is the first of many shameless plugs for the author's previous book.

just the same.

And then I think back to December of 1998, and recall how the press whipped the people into a frenzy by literally *demanding* the further mass bombing of Iraq. Saddam had not learned his lesson, we were told, and needed a further show of America's resolve to enforce 'humanitarian' standards and the 'rule of law.'

And so a nation that had just a decade before been the most socially advanced in the Middle East, with the highest literacy rate and the best schools, the best healthcare and quality of life, and the most advanced civilian infrastructure—and which now was reduced to abject poverty and rampant disease—would once again be bombed.

Once again toxic agents such as depleted uranium would be rained down indiscriminately. And once again chemical sites on the ground would be targeted, poisoning the land and the air, threatening food and water supplies, and killing the hopes and dreams of the Iraqi people that *their* children wouldn't be joining their friends and classmates who had already perished.

And, sadly, once again the American people would cheer.

That, my friends, is what you would call belligerent nationalism. A considerably more benign example of this phenomenon is the practice of sending a bunch of arrogant professional basketball players dubbed the 'Dream Team' to, say, the Olympic Games, and then swelling with patriotic pride when they then predictably thrash their opponents, signaling to the world that America reigns supreme.

Yet another example could be, for instance, using a lost, bewildered and traumatized six-year-old Cuban boy as a political football to demonstrate our superiority to a 'rogue state.' All of which seems to suggest that we have the *belligerent nationalism* thing pretty well nailed down. We're now two-for-two and ready to examine the next component – *racism*.

This one seems like pretty much of a slam-dunk. The 500-year-in-the-making genocide of Native Americans[3] and the enslavement of African-Americans for nearly the first century of the country's existence would seem to suggest that America has built a solid historical foundation as one of the most racist nations on Earth.

The fact that even after the slaves were emancipated, black Americans were not granted their civil rights for another entire century, and even then only after violent uprisings, would tend to bolster that conclusion. But is America an overtly racist society even today? Unfortunately, the facts would tend to indicate that this is indeed the case.

For example, there is an enormous gap in the incarceration rates for white and black Americans, with African Americans being at least six times more likely to be under the physical control of the state.[4] And Hispanics fare little better in the US criminal justice system. The standard conservative response to this indisputable fact is that ethnic minorities are just far more likely to commit crimes — they in fact constitute a 'criminal element' in society.

This is, however, a convenient justification that purposefully ignores how the system actually functions. The truth is that the incidence of reported crime in this country does not vary widely by race. It has been reported, for instance, that while African Americans constitute just 12% of the US population, and a nearly

---

[3]   The best book on this topic is David E. Stannard's *American Holocaust,* Oxford University Press, 1992. Stannard's research indicates that the total death toll of Native Americans could well exceed 100,000,000.

[4]   *U.S. Department of Justice Bulletin NCJ170014,* August 1998

identical percentage of the illegal drug-using population (13%), a full 74% of those people imprisoned for drug possession are black.[5]

The discrepancy by race in the rates of punitive measures taken by the state is actually a product of a system of criminal justice that is largely a discretionary system, with many actors wielding the power to determine how a case will ultimately be disposed of, and with the race of the accused playing a key role throughout the process.[6]

For instance, the first point of contact for most Americans with the justice system is generally with the police, who have a range of options for penalizing an offender. The cop can choose—among other options—to issue a warning, issue a citation, or to make an arrest. Conventional wisdom to the contrary, which of these options is chosen is frequently not dependent on the severity of the offense, but by characteristics of the suspect that are unrelated to the crime, notably his or her race.

Once taken into custody (if the officer on the street opts to make an arrest), other law enforcement officers have the option of booking the offender or merely detaining him or her. A prosecutor then has the discretionary power to decide which charges, if any, to file against the accused, and this same prosecutor further has the authority to lessen those charges in exchange for a guilty plea from the defendant.

---

[5] National Criminal Justice Commission, February 1996

[6] This has been documented most recently in a report issued on May 4, 2000 by the Washington, D.C.-based Leadership Council on Civil Rights - a fifty-year-old alliance of 185 human rights groups - entitled "Justice on Trial: Racial Disparities in the American Criminal Justice System" (Erin Texeira "Justice Is Not Colorblind, Studies Find," *Los Angeles Times,* May 22, 2000).

Further on in the process, if the accused is found to be guilty, the prosecutor and/or the judge has the discretion to determine the sentence – ranging from a fine or community service to prison time or even death. While this is a simplified view of the machinations of the American criminal justice system, the point is that there are several steps along the way where the law is superceded by the discretionary power of various actors.

And at each of the steps along the way, African Americans and other minority defendants fare far worse than do white criminal suspects. Blacks are far more likely to be arrested, given the same circumstances of the crime, than are Whites. Once arrested, Blacks are much more likely to be charged with serious crimes than are Whites. And of course Blacks are more likely to be convicted in court, and to receive a harsher sentence upon conviction.

It is not uncommon, in fact, for a black youth to be processed completely through the system and receive prison time for an offense for which a white youth would have been let off with a warning or a citation.[7] And continuing with this pattern, African Americans are much more likely to be denied parole or to have strict conditions placed upon their parole. Such is the racist nature of the American criminal justice system.

Yet this is not the only manifestation of racism in America today. There is also the fact that Native Americans remain the

---

[7] The venerable *Los Angeles Times* has reported, for instance, that: "A black youth is six times more likely to be locked up than a white peer, even when charged with a similar crime and when neither has a prior record ... Minority youth are more likely than white youth who commit comparable crimes to be referred to juvenile court, be detained, face trial as adults and be jailed with adults" ("Black Youth Face Bias in Justice System," *Los Angeles Times,* April 26, 2000).

most oppressed and victimized ethnic group in the US today, with by far the lowest living standards and the highest rates of victimization by crime, as well as incarceration rates even higher than that of black males.[8]

There is also the uncomfortable fact that during the Reagan administration, not too many years ago, top aides—including Lt. Col. Oliver North—drafted contingency plans that included the mass internment of black Americans in concentration camps.[9] This was, of course, at the very same time that cheap crack cocaine—entering the country with the complicity of the CIA[10]— was systematically devastating 'inner city' neighborhoods.

Add to this the fact that during those same 1980's the United States consistently voted, in defiance of world opinion and any sense of decency, *against* all attempts to impose sanctions on the Apartheid regime in South Africa,[11] and it begins to look like this isn't exactly an era of racial enlightenment in America.

Then there is the issue of immigrant bashing — long a favorite pastime in California, particularly under the governorship of Pete Wilson. Of course, there are other manifestations of racism as well—perhaps most notably the precipitous rise in the number of hate groups being spawned across the country—but suffice it to say that the available evidence strongly suggests that America is still firmly committed to the racist principles on which it was founded.

---

8 *Derailing Democracy,* chapter 11
9 "Reagan Advisers Ran Secret Government," *Miami Herald,* July 5, 1987
10 Gary Webb *Dark Alliance,* Seven Stories Press, 1998
11 William Blum "The U.S. Versus the World at the United Nations," in *Rogue State,* Common Courage Press, 2000

If there is any lingering doubt of that, one has only to take a look at the composition of the US Senate and the White House team at any given time, or at the rosters of the *Forbes* or the *Fortune 500* lists. It's readily apparent in doing so that unless your name is Oprah Winfrey or Colin Powell, America's corridors of power are still pretty much of a 'whites only' club.

So it seems fairly safe to say that we can check *racism* off the list and move on to component number six – *militarism*. This one is an absolute no-brainer, given that the US is without question the most heavily militarized nation ever to take up residence on planet Earth. The United States currently spends more on what we euphemistically term 'defense,' in fact, than the rest of the UN Security Council combined. And that's just with what we openly acknowledge as military spending.

This does not include, for example, much of the CIA's unaccountable 'black' budget—variously estimated to be between $50 and $100 billion annually—a huge portion of which is used for covert military operations. Nor does it include the funding of 'civilian' entities such as NASA, which masquerade as non-military agencies when in fact they are an integral part of the military/intelligence infrastructure of this country.

Also not included is the funding for the arming and training of foreign forces, which often masquerades as non-military, 'humanitarian assistance.' This assistance, it should be noted, is rarely if ever offered for the benefit of the host country, but rather to extend the reach of the US military, primarily for the benefit of an increasingly small sector of corporate America.

When all of what actually constitutes military spending is tallied up, the truth is that America very likely spends more on 'defense' than the entire rest of the world combined.[12] By doing so, we long ago achieved absolute naval superiority over the world's oceans. We also maintain the ability to establish air superiority anywhere in the world at any time we should so choose. And of course, we have for decades had unquestioned nuclear superiority.

Yet even all of this is not enough. Now our military leaders desire to have absolute military superiority in *space*,[13] policing the world with an interlinked system of satellites encompassing the globe, able to strike without warning anywhere in the world. And just in case that proves an inadequate level of military control, other explicitly stated or implied goals include controlling the planet's weather and food supply for military purposes.[14]

America has become increasingly militarized in another way as well, alarmingly so in the last decade, as the line has steadily been blurred between the military and civilian police agencies.[15] This domestic militarization is perhaps even more ominous than is the militarization of foreign policy, which has arguably always been based primarily on brute force.

It has become increasingly difficult to discern any difference between the training, the weaponry and the tactics employed by the nation's domestic police forces and its military services. Police now routinely patrol America's streets—particularly in the euphemistically termed 'inner cities'—in military-style helicopters and armored personnel carriers, brandishing military-issue automatic weapons, as well as the occasional grenade launcher and a host of other military 'surplus' equipment.

---

[12] Michael Parenti *Against Empire*, City Lights Books, 1995

[13] *Derailing Democracy*, chapter 30

[14] *Derailing Democracy*, chapters 12 and 31

[15] Christian Parenti's *Lockdown America* (Verso Books, 1999) provides a look at the militarization of the police over the last few decades.

Paramilitary police squads, or SWAT units—originally a creation of the Los Angeles Police Department—are now an integral part of nearly every police agency in the country. Perhaps to up the ante just a bit, that same LAPD has now given an even more militarized and brutal model to the country – the infamously corrupt CRASH units.

A parallel trend in recent years has been the increasingly close coordination between federal, state and local law enforcement bodies, all in the name of fighting terrorism on America's shores. The end result, which does not appear to be too far in the distance, is the creation of a unified and highly militarized national police force.

It's safe to say then that we can check militarism off the list. We've now confirmed four of the original six components of *fascism*, with just two more to go. We're already two-thirds of the way there. But now we must return to the two more debatable factors that we conveniently skipped over initially.

Those factors, for those who have forgotten, are the notions of *a one-party dictatorship* and of *forcible suppression of opposition*. And here, you may believe, is where the argument that America is a fascist state falls apart. For surely America is not a one-party state—let alone a dictatorship—nor do we forcibly suppress opposition.

These facts are plainly evident to any observer of the American ship of state. But do these seemingly self-evident facts represent an objective reality, or a carefully crafted and maintained illusion? Put forth another way, is the existence of various competing political parties and ideologies merely an elaborate hoax that has successfully pulled the wool over America's eyes?

Chapter 3

The One-Party State?

The commercial press, in another of its brazen hypocritical proclamations, points with pride to the fact that it is free because it upholds a free system in which there are two political parties. But there is probably not one member of the A.N.P.A. [American Newspaper Publishers Association] who does not know that the Republican and Democratic parties both feed out of the same bag provided by the monied system, and that the same persons frequently subscribe funds to both major parties ... They know this very well, and they also know very well that the press has never given honest news coverage to the formation, platform and campaign of any third party which was independent enough not to feed on the same money.

George Seldes, 1943

First of all, we all know that America is not a one-party state; it's a two-party state. Or maybe three, if you count Ross Perot's Reform Party, though precisely what it is about the current system that they intend to 'reform' is not exactly clear.

What should be abundantly clear to any rational-minded American by this time is that there is absolutely no substantive difference between the two major political parties in this country. This has been noted with increasing frequency by various writers, who have dubbed the emerging one-size-fits-all party the Republicrats.

It is my belief, in fact, that the Republican and Democratic Parties do not actually exist. And the notion that the US federal government operates as some sort of give-and-take between the Democratic/liberal agenda, and the Republican/conservative agenda, is pure fantasy.

This is not to suggest that among the people in this nation who consider themselves Democrats or Republicans there are no legitimate differences of opinion. Most certainly there are. But I *am* suggesting that at the highest levels of government, where the agenda setting power lies, there is no such thing as a Democratic agenda and a Republican agenda – there is only *the* agenda, and the only debate is over how rapidly that agenda can be implemented while still maintaining the illusion of democracy.

And make no mistake about it, maintaining the illusion is of paramount importance. That is why it is essential that prominent men with virtually identical ideologies must pretend to be political rivals and to deeply despise one another. The bitter bipartisanship that ripples through Washington on a regular basis assures us that differing viewpoints are being heard, and that at least some of those in Washington represent *our* point of view.

Indeed, were it not for the relentless attacks upon Bill Clinton by the rabid right-wingers that have dogged him since his taking office, how would we even know that Clinton was a liberal? You would certainly be hard-pressed to ascertain that fact from the record of his administration.

Oh sure, he fooled us at first. We all saw how hip he was blowing his sax on Arsenio's late-night show and dancing to Fleetwood Mac at his inauguration. We all heard him deny that he had inhaled, though of course we all knew that he had. And we all heard about how he had protested the Vietnam War — on foreign soil no less. Hell, this guy was so liberal he was practically guilty of treason.

And we had hope in the early days of his administration as he set about as though he was going to reform healthcare and address the issue of gays in the military. But then a funny thing happened. After faltering on both of those issues, the Clinton administration quickly set about implementing the most reactionary agenda of any president in modern history.

In fact, Clinton has instituted 'reforms' that remained mere wet dreams for his Republican predecessors, including the decimation of the welfare system. He has done more to militarize the nation's police forces than any president in history. By the time he leaves office, the number of Americans incarcerated will have nearly doubled during his time in office.[16]

The use of the death penalty has skyrocketed during his tenure, with its use expanded to cover more crimes, and with appeals of death penalty cases severely limited. His time in office has also seen the country increasingly execute juvenile offenders, and increasingly incarcerate minors as adults.

Privatization of prisons, a movement that was just taking baby steps under the Reagan and Bush administrations, has flourished under Clinton. So too has the use of inmate labor by private corporations as a form of ersatz slave labor[17] (the vast majority of Nazi Germany's concentration camps were, by the way, privately

---

16 As the *Associated Press* reported on February 18, 2001 (Karen Gullo "Study Shows Prisons Filled at Record Pace in Clinton Years"): "More Americans went to prison or jail during the Clinton administration than during any past administration, the result of get-tough policies that led to more prisons, more police officers and longer sentences." The Justice Policy Institute reported that the incarceration rate at the end of Clinton's terms of office was nearly double what it had been at the end of Reagan's terms – 476 per 100,000 vs. 247 per 100,000.

17 Information on the current state of America's police and prisons can be found in *Derailing Democracy* and in Christian Parenti's *Lockdown America*.

owned slave labor camps. Auschwitz, for example, was con-
structed by I.G. Farben and its business partner, Standard Oil, to
provide a steady source of disposable labor).

The sales of arms to foreign regimes—already at a high level
during the Bush administration—doubled in Clinton's first year in
office alone.[18] And the militarization of foreign policy has far
surpassed what the belligerent Bush team was able to achieve. In
one seven month period, the Clinton White House conducted aerial bombing and/or cruise missile assaults against no fewer than
four sovereign nations: Iraq, Serbia, Afghanistan, and the Sudan.
All of these were conducted in rather flagrant disregard for international law.

Clinton has also—aside from conducting a full scale war of his
own in Yugoslavia—continued George Bush's punitive war
against Iraq. By the time he leaves office, well over a million Iraqis
will have died on his watch, considerably more than were killed in
the initial air war by his predecessor.

In Haiti and Somalia as well, Clinton has shown a willingness,
an eagerness even, to use military force. He has also presided over
an unprecedented erosion of the judicial system and a vast under-
mining of privacy rights.[19] Social spending has become almost
non-existent and the Dow Jones has become the only relevant economic indicator.

Clinton has also been an unapologetic backer of 'globalization.'
Whether it's NAFTA or GATT or the WTO, this administration

---

[18] "U.S. Arms Sales: Arms Around the World," *The Mojo Wire*
[19] *Derailing Democracy,* chapters 22 and 23

has never met a 'free trade' bill or organization it didn't like. Wealth has been concentrated during Clinton's tenure on a scale never before seen in history, as the gap between rich and poor widens with each passing week.

As for the enforcement of anti-trust legislation, forget it. The show trial of Microsoft notwithstanding, this administration has allowed the biggest mergers in history, with each year continuing to set new records — most recently with the joining of Time-Warner and AOL. Environmental protections? None to be seen. Labor standards and protections? Not likely.

The truth about the record of this administration is that any Republican on earth would be delighted to leave office with such a legacy. Clinton has without a doubt been the best friend in Washington that the 'conservatives' could have ever hoped for — which brings up the obvious question of why so many of them have such an apparent disdain for the man.

The first answer which came to mind when pondering this question was that they were just jealous of Bill for being a better Republican than they are. And then, as if suddenly struck by a divine insight, it came to me. I now know the answer to the question of why the conservatives in Washington hate Bill Clinton.

The answer is that there is no answer to that question because it is not a valid question, due to the fact that it is based on a false premise. For the dirty little secret is that the right-wingers *don't* hate Bill Clinton. They love the guy. And why shouldn't they? He has, after all, pursued 'their' agenda, and done so with nary a whimper of protest from the American left.

But why then, the question is begged, has the Republican Right done everything in its power to discredit, embarrass, and bring about the early demise of this administration? Because, strange as it may initially sound, that is precisely *why* Clinton has been so successful in pursuing such a reactionary agenda.

The truth of the matter is that without the constant broadsides launched at the White House, Clinton would have long ago ceased to pass for anything remotely resembling a liberal. Those on the political left who initially supported the new administration would have quickly abandoned the course it chose to follow. The only reason that Clinton has held the support of these factions, as well as of more mainstream Democrats for that matter, is precisely *because of* the constant attacks.

After all, the reasoning goes, if he is so thoroughly despised by the most intolerant right-wing extremists on Capitol Hill, then surely he *must* be a liberal. At the very least, one is left to conclude, he is the lesser of two evils, and any enemy of *those guys* must surely be an ally of mine.

And so this president has held the support of centrists and leftists alike, even as he has waged acts of war around the world, gutted domestic spending, given no more than lip service to social issues, and facilitated the rise of the prosecutorial police state. Even those who seriously question the policies of Clinton have surmised that things could only be worse with a Republican in the White House.

This may well be a false notion. The truth could very well be that we have fared considerably worse with a 'Democrat,' for it is precisely because Clinton is perceived as such that he has 'succeeded' in areas in which his Republican predecessors had failed. A Republican president, for instance, would not have been able to destroy the welfare state without invoking the wrath of the American people.

Neither would he be able to routinely wage acts of war, seemingly on a whim. Lefties are instinctively on alert for such shenanigans by Republican presidents. But when a 'liberal' embarks on such missions, we tend to give him the benefit of the doubt, even when that liberal is actually a conservative Republican.

In retrospect, we should have known something was amiss right away. A rather odd, but seemingly trivial aspect of the 1992 presidential campaign that brought Clinton to power should have signaled to the people that something wasn't quite right about the American political landscape.

The event referred to actually occurred after the close of the campaign, when the bright lights were mostly turned away. That was when Clinton's campaign manager, James Carville, and Bush's campaign manager, Mary Matalin—who had just conducted a no-holds barred, anything goes, win-at-all-costs mudfest—decided to cap off the campaign by getting married.

Nothing unusual about that, right? We all know that opposites attract. Even when those opposites have just devoted a considerable amount of energy to, by appearances anyway, completely destroying the reputations and careers of the other's candidate and campaign team. Even when those opposites are allegedly fiercely opposed to the other's ideology and have absolutely no respect for the integrity of the other's mission.

It does seem just a bit odd, however, that two such opposites would even have the *opportunity* to attract one another in the course of such a vicious campaign. How is it even possible that they could have interacted on a level that would have fostered a personal, let alone an intimate, relationship?

Unless, that is, the adversarial nature of this particular campaign, and of political campaigns in general, was largely an illusion — a sham foisted on the people to foster the perception that the American political system is based on deep divisions between competing political parties and ideologies.

This is precisely why nearly all political campaigns for major office in this country quickly degenerate into mud-slinging contests. In truth, this is the only way that the illusion of diversity can be maintained. The real issues are rarely discussed because, quite frankly, there is nothing *to* discuss.

All of the 'major party' candidates are in agreement on all the issues of any real significance. They cannot differentiate between themselves and create the illusion of a meaningful choice to voters by discussing issues on which they all agree, and so they agree to disagree on a few largely inconsequential issues, and throw up a smokescreen of salacious allegations.

In this way, it is hoped, the voting public will be deceived into believing that they are being offered a legitimate choice between competing ideologies. For surely there must be marked differences between these men, or why else would they hate each other so?

The truth is that they hate one another only in the sense that 'professional' wrestlers hate their rivals. I hate to be the one to pull the curtain back on the wizard, but it's all for show, folks. When the lights go up and the curtain drops down, they're all friends again.

In the case of the aforementioned 1992 election contest between George Bush and Bill Clinton, for example, abundant evidence has been presented by researchers that suggests that the two bitter 'rivals' had a rather cozy relationship extending back to Clinton's days as governor of Arkansas.[20]

It seems that the good governor was considerate enough to allow his state to be used as a base for George and Ollie's illegal Contra operations. From an airfield in Mena, Arkansas, weapons

---

[20] See, for example, Terry Reed and John Cummings' *Compromised* (Penmarin Books, 1995), and Alexander Cockburn and Jeffrey St. Clair's *Whiteout* (Verso Books, 1998).

were flown out of the country and drugs were flown back in. This, of course, required the full knowledge and protection of the governor's office, especially when the Contra team began flying recruits in for training in a covert training camp.

These types of operations tend to involve a lot of cash, and this one was no exception. Some of this naturally found its way into the hands of the governor. Luckily the Rose Law Firm, where his wife and good friends Web Hubbell and Vince Foster happened to work, was very good at laundering these types of soiled profits.

But Bill Clinton earned more than just some extra cash from his complicity in this sordid affair. More importantly, he also gained important connections to George Bush and his inner circle, and very likely earned the right to pose as the Democratic candidate in the 1992 election.

Bill Clinton's role in that election campaign, essentially, was as an insurance policy for the Bush camp. Clinton was propped up as the 'Democratic' alternative to Bush in the event that the electorate sought a more 'liberal' alternative to the then-current administration.

In reality, the choice faced by voters in the 1992 election was between the real George Bush and the George Bush surrogate named Bill Clinton. The only change in the agenda seems to have been an acceleration in the erosion of democratic rights under the cover of a 'liberal' administration.

I am not suggesting here, mind you, that the 1992 election was unusual, in the sense that there was something that set it apart from other presidential elections, or from most gubernatorial and congressional elections, for that matter. I'm actually suggesting that they are all pretty much of a sham.

That's why it shouldn't have surprised anyone to see President Clinton, following his 2000 State of the Union address, walking arm-in-arm with former Klansman Strom Thurmond and glad-handing some of the most openly fascistic elements of the US government, men who had just the year before been all but calling for his public execution.

And it also shouldn't surprise anyone when the losers in any given primary campaign predictably endorse and embrace the candidacy of the party front-runner, even when those same losers had previously denounced their party rival as the spawn of Satan. They all know that it's just a game and that all will be forgiven.

Of course the press will feign amazement over how quickly the bitter divisions have been mended, but they too know how the game is played; they just don't want to spoil the fun for the rest of us. So they play along, and try to paint as stark a contrast between the opposing candidates as they can.

Chapter 4

Bringing Out the Big Guns

The best way to safeguard a secret is to pretend to share it with others.
maxim of long-time CIA Director Allen W. Dulles

One of the clearest indications of the fraudulent nature of election campaigns in this country is the fact that the 'big guns,' so to speak, are routinely withheld. In other words, while there is undoubtedly a torrent of mud tossed back and forth, the really good mud clods (you know, the ones with the rocks inside) are never thrown.

In the case of the previously discussed 1992 election, the reason for that is pretty clear. All of the best mud, the mud that could really do some damage (i.e., the Contra mud), tended to soil both the Democratic and Republican contenders for president. Neither campaign could expose the other's role without implicating themselves. But that is not always the case.

There are any number of examples of candidacies that could have been shot down — but the knockout punch never surfaced. Of course, sometimes it does surface, as was the case with the Dukakis campaign and the Willie Horton issue, or the Gary Hart campaign and the Donna Rice episode. But this fate seems to befall mostly those candidates who are unqualified to occupy the White House anyway, in that they don't fully understand the rules of the game.

It also befalls those candidates who, though aware of the rules of play, nevertheless stand in the way of the preordained winner. If such a candidate proves to be too popular, he will need to be replaced by someone who actually makes the chosen one look good, relatively speaking. This is not the case with a candidate such as George W. Bush though. George is a chip off the old block – a good team player and, by all appearances, the chosen successor to the throne.

That is why it is very unlikely that any cruise-missile mud clods will be fired his way. This is, mind you, despite the fact that George W. has a Willie Horton in his closet that would put Michael Dukakis to shame. Or maybe you hadn't heard about George's act of compassionate conservatism? It seems that the governor took some unusual actions in June of 1998 that have yet to be aired. But first, a little background on Bush's term as governor.

As of this writing, Texas' smirking governor has cleared the way for 150 executions of convicted inmates. That is more, it should be noted, than any governor in any state in the history of the nation. That's not a bad record for being in office for less than six years. And he still has more time to kill (pardon the pun) as governor.

Now this does not likely register as a negative with Bush's conservative base. They love a guy who is tough on crime. It's not even a negative that some of those executed were mentally impaired and/or mentally ill, nor that some of them had credible claims of innocence.[21] Nor even that two of them were women – two of only five women executed in the entire country in the last quarter-century.

---

[21] An independent investigation by the *Chicago Tribune* concluded that "Under Gov. George W. Bush, Texas has executed dozens of Death Row inmates whose cases were compromised by unreliable evidence, disbarred or suspended defense attorneys, meager defense efforts during sentencing and dubious psychiatric testimony." Of the 131 cases reviewed, 23 of the convictions were based at least in part on the testimony of jailhouse informants, 43 involved defense attorneys publicly sanctioned for misconduct, 29 included psychiatric testimony condemned as unethical and untrustworthy by the American Psychiatric Association, and 40 of the condemned men were represented by defense attorneys who either presented no evidence or called but a single witness during the sentencing phase of the trial (Steve Mills, Ken Armstrong and Douglas Holt "Flawed Trials Lead to Death Chamber: Bush Confident in System Rife with Problems," *Chicago Tribune,* June 11, 2000).

Most of Bush's core constituents would likewise not be bothered by the fact that some of those executed were convicted of crimes committed as minors. It's good to be tough on crime. When Bill Clinton was running for president, he made a point of running home to Arkansas to sign off on the execution of Ricky Ray Rector, a man so severely retarded that when guards had to interrupt his last meal to lead him to his execution, he reportedly assured them that he would just have to finish when they got back.

And it was good that Clinton did that. One can never be too tough on crime, even when one is a liberal Democrat. That is why it is so unusual that Governor Bush, with his first national election looming, did what he did. For you see, George, Jr. doesn't have a perfect score on his execution record.

While 150 executions have been carried out in the state of Texas under his watch, 151 cases have come before the governor for review. Only one of them was deemed worthy of clemency (Bush has issued only one *stay* of execution as well, in order for the case to be reviewed. Following the review, the inmate—Ricky Nolen McGinn—was executed). The rather obvious question begged here is: who was the recipient of Governor Bush's compassionate conservatism? [22]

A good first guess might be Betty Lou Beets, the great-grandmother in her sixties who was convicted of killing her husband after years of violent physical abuse. That, alas, would be a wrong

---

[22] *The Mojo Wire* reported on December 23, 1999 (Vince Beiser "Wasted Youth") that: "Texas' Bush has also commuted only one death sentence," though the story notably failed to identify who the recipient of that commutation was.

guess. She was walked down the aisle and strapped onto the table on February 24 of 2000. The correct answer is—drum roll please—Henry Lee Lucas.

Henry is, for the uninformed, the most prolific, and arguably the most brutal, serial killer in the annals of crime. If his confessions and the accounts of various law enforcement personnel are to be believed, Henry and his sometime cohort Ottis Toole are responsible for between 300 and 600 serial slayings.

And these were not, mind you, your garden variety killings. Henry is a necrophile and torture aficionado, while his partner was a confessed arsonist and cannibal. Their victims were frequently tortured, sexually abused before and after death, mutilated and dismembered, cannibalized, beheaded, and subjected to any other depraved urges the pair could conjure up.

There was an even darker aspect to many of their crimes. Just for kicks, Henry and Ottis liked to bring along Toole's niece and nephew on their killing sprees. The two youngsters, aged just 10 and 11 when their forced collaboration began, were forced to witness and sometimes participate in the torture, killing, and mutilation of victims.

So if one were to play the Devil's advocate in favor of the death penalty, it would be pretty difficult to find a better poster boy for the justness of judicial executions. If ever there were a man for whom the ultimate punishment was intended, Henry would have to be it. If his confessed death toll is accurate, Henry is responsible for wreaking more death and misery on the nation than the other 150 convicts sent to the execution chamber by Governor Bush combined, even assuming that they were all actually guilty of the crimes for which they were convicted.

More deaths also than Ted Bundy, Jeffrey Dahmer, John Wayne Gacy, Richard Ramirez, Charles Manson and a few other of America's celebrity serial killers combined – which makes it very unusual that Henry's life was spared by America's premier hanging governor.

Even more unusual—but only if one accepts that political campaigns are legitimate contests between rivals—is the fact that no one has bothered to mention this whole affair. It's not hard to imagine the damage to Bush's core support that this story could cause. Any one of Bush's Republican Primary opponents could have attacked him on the issue.

And yet all remained silent. Steve Forbes, Orrin Hatch, Alan Keyes, Gary Bauer, and others whose names I have already forgotten, chose not to wield this sword. Even John McCain, allegedly locked in a bitter struggle for the support of the party faithful, chose not to play the Henry Lee card. There is virtually no chance that Gore will choose to do so in the general election campaign.

But had I been given just one week running the campaign of any of Bush's rivals, Democrat or Republican, George would have been out of the race – guaranteed. I can already picture the Willie Horton-style campaign ads saturating the country. As the announcer solemnly recounts how Governor Bush made a special request to Texas' Board of Pardons to review Henry's case and then proceeded to commute Henry's death sentence, a roll call of Henry's victims scrolls endlessly across the screen.

There they are for all the voters to see, all the shattered lives— young and old, men, women, and children—hundreds of them flashing across the screen. And then at the end, a shot of Henry sitting comfortably in his cell. Maybe we could even coax him into uttering a "thanks Governor" for the camera. As soon as someone sends me the money, I'll start filming the spot.

None of this is meant to suggest that I think the state of Texas should have killed Henry Lee Lucas. Nor do I think that it is a good idea to run political campaign spots advocating blood lust.

Rather, the Henry Lee Lucas story is told here to illustrate that what appears to be full scale political warfare is in reality very selective and tightly controlled mud-slinging (and to highlight the ridiculously arbitrary nature of the application of the death penalty).

Some issues are clearly off-limits and Henry, it would appear, is one of them. It should be noted here that it is not just Bush's political rivals that have avoided turning Henry Lee Lucas into this year's Willie Horton. The press has completely ignored the story as well, though this is hardly surprising.

Well, you may be thinking, that's an interesting little story, but is it enough to derail the candidacy of George, Jr.? Not to worry – I have a back-up plan. Should the Henry Lee story fail to generate an adequate amount of outrage among the voters, there is always the possibility of excavating some old mud on a particularly unsavory aspect of the Bush family history.

Since all is fair in a down-and-dirty election campaign, I see no reason why we shouldn't hold George accountable for the sins of his fathers. To do so, we need to look back to the year 1942, admittedly before the current Bush family candidate was even born. But that's OK. Guilt by association is a valid part of any good mud-slinging campaign.

1942 was, as many readers will recall, the year that America made its belated entrance into WWII. The US actually declared war in December of 1941, but it was well into 1942 before American troops joined the fighting, primarily at first in the Pacific theater of operations. It would not be until June of 1944, two and a half years later, that the US would muster any serious resistance to the Nazi menace in Europe, even though we entered the war with a stated policy of 'Europe First.' But we'll have to get back to that later.

The ostensible reason for our entry into the war, it will be remembered, was the attack on Pearl Harbor on December 7,

1941. Strangely enough, this attack came *the morning after* a massive counterattack was launched by the Red Army to repel the hordes of Nazi troops running amok through much of the western half of the Soviet Union.[23]

Prior to this counteroffensive, it was widely assumed that the Germans would soundly defeat the Soviet forces. And the Americans didn't much care. They didn't really want to get involved, just as they didn't want to get involved as the German troops had plowed through Czechoslovakia, Poland, Hungary, Romania, Bulgaria, Yugoslavia, Belgium, France, Holland, Greece, and Norway as they set about creating a continuous 1,800 mile front on which to attack the Soviet Union.

With the launching of the Soviet counteroffensive, however, America suddenly took a keen interest in the affairs of its European neighbors. It suddenly became apparent that the Red Army, unlike most of those previously encountered by the Axis forces, was actually going to fight back and, most likely, ultimately defeat the German Army.

And if that were to happen, our Russian 'allies' might even decide to roll on through Western Europe, doing a more thorough job of denazifying the region than some Westerners had in mind. So it was a good thing that the Japanese launched such a timely attack on Pearl Harbor, giving the US the necessary pretext for jumping into the fray.[24]

---

[23] The *Encyclopaedia Britannica* notes the dates that these two events occurred. Like other modern histories of the war, however, events occurring on the Western Front are presented in a separate narrative from events occurring on the Eastern Front. The effect, of course, is to imply to the reader that there were no connections between these events.

[24] Interestingly, as this book was being written, a new book was released by the Free Press, Robert S. Stinnett's *Day of Deceit*. Stinnett provides documentation just uncovered and never before published indicating that Pearl Harbor was indeed an event carefully orchestrated by the U.S. government to justify America's entry into the war at a time of its choosing.

But we'll have to get back to that later as well. The point is that by 1942, America was in a fully declared state of war with Japan and the European Axis powers. And it was in that same year that the United States Alien Property Custodian, acting under authority of the Trading With the Enemy Act, seized the assets of several subsidiaries of the Wall Street powerhouse of Brown Bothers/Harriman.[25]

These subsidiaries, including the Union Banking Co. and the Hamburg-Amerika Shipping Line, were declared to be operating as Nazi fronts, which is exactly what they do appear to have been. The problem here for the current presidential candidate is that two of the principals of Brown Brothers were none other than Prescott Bush and Herbert Walker (along with Averell Harriman). That would be the father and grandfather of former president George Bush, and the grandfather and great-grandfather of future president George W. Bush.

This was not, by any means, the only group of bankers and industrialists who were actively trading with and financing the fascist powers of Europe.[26] But it does raise rather serious questions as to the source of the Bush family's considerable wealth. Even so, it is an issue that has not, and will not, be raised in the current presidential campaign, just as it was not an issue that was raised in any of George, Sr.'s runs for political office.

Neither was it an issue that prevented Prescott Bush from becoming one of the most influential senators in the country and

---

[25] See *The Secret War Against the Jews* (St. Martin's Press, 1994) by Mark Aarons and former Justice Department investigator John Loftus.

[26] See, for example, Charles Higham's *Trading With the Enemy*, Delacorte Press, 1983. Higham provides documentation of the collaboration with Nazi Germany by a number of industrial and financial concerns, including Ford Motors, General Motors, ITT, RCA, the Rockefeller family's Standard Oil and Chase Bank, and many others. The research of John Loftus has revealed that fully 70% of the financing of the Third Reich came from American and British investors.

an advisor to President Eisenhower. That's because politicians and media outlets who understand how the game is played don't raise such troubling issues.

In the unlikely event that these two issues would fail to crush young George's political aspirations, there is yet a third skeleton in the Bush closet that could do some serious damage not just to George W., but to George H.W. as well – but we're saving that for chapter 6.

To summarize then what has become a rather long and rambling diatribe: there are no actual major political parties in this country (a fact greatly elaborated on in Part II of this book), and election campaigns consist largely of a bunch of guys in expensive suits pretending to be bitter rivals when they are actually all playing on the same team. That, in a nutshell, is how the American political system works.

All of this may sound just a little bit implausible to many readers. How then, you may well ask, are we to explain the impeachment of our beloved 'liberal' president? An excellent question – and one that will require a new chapter to examine.

Chapter 5

Impeachment – or Prelude to War?

The size of a lie is a definite factor in causing it to be believed, because the vast masses of a nation are in the depths of their hearts more easily deceived than they are consciously and intentionally bad. The primitive simplicity of their minds renders them more easy victims of a big lie than a small one, because they themselves often tell little lies but would be ashamed to tell big ones. Such a form of lying would never enter their heads. They would never credit others with the possibility of such great impudence as the complete reversal of facts.
Adolf Hitler, 1923

If ever there was an event that demonstrated the deep divisions between the 'liberals' and the 'conservatives' on Capitol Hill, then surely it was the impeachment of President Clinton. Certainly this event disproved the ludicrous notion that there are no competing political parties or ideologies in this country. Or did it?

There are two general points of view among the people in this country on the impeachment fiasco. One is that it was a legitimate and lawful effort to rid the country of a thoroughly corrupt head of state whose 'liberal' values had brought shame and disgrace upon the White House and the nation.

The other is that it was a totally unwarranted attack whose goal was to depose a legally elected and popular president, through whatever means were necessary to do so. I would suggest that neither interpretation is correct, though the latter point of view is an accurate description of what *appeared* to occur.

But what appeared to occur is not necessarily what actually did occur. I would suggest that it is entirely plausible that the whole affair was a sham, a carefully stage-managed event from start to finish. Preposterous, you say? For what possible purpose would such an elaborate event be concocted? Glad you asked.

There are actually any number of reasons for putting on the Bill and Monica stage show. For one, the impeachment of Clinton, more than any other single event, established his unquestioned standing as a liberal. What other explanation could there be for such a vicious, lengthy, and unrelenting attack upon the beleaguered president by the likes of Trent Lott, Henry Hyde, Bob Barr, Tom DeLay and Newt Gingrich?

One possible explanation could be precisely to create the *illusion* of deep divisions between Republican and Democratic factions. After all, after five years of pursuing an increasingly reactionary agenda, there was a danger of Clinton's facade beginning to slip. Poor Bill's poll numbers were beginning to drop.

This is not, of course, unusual for a second term president, but was entirely unacceptable what with the US having a war to wage just over the horizon. And a war, if waged overtly, requires a reasonable level of support from the American people in order to be waged successfully.

And this war, in particular, had only the flimsiest of pretenses on which to sell it to the American people, so it required that the people be, in general terms, solidly behind their president prior to the commencement of hostilities – and also that the people be caught off-guard, so to speak.

If they accomplished nothing else, the impeachment proceedings marshaled forth an unprecedented level of support for a second-term president. Conventional wisdom, of course, tells us that this was precisely the opposite effect intended by his Republican pursuers. Yet at each step of the long and tedious process, Clinton's poll numbers continued to rise.

When the infamous Starr Report was posted on the internet, his numbers went up. When the videotape of his deposition in the Paula Jones case was aired *ad naseum*, his numbers went up again. When the House Judiciary Committee voted out articles of impeachment, his numbers continued to climb. When the full House voted out two of those same articles, his numbers again went up.

By the time the proceedings reached the Senate, and that solemn body opted to hold limited hearings, Clinton's poll numbers were reaching for the stratosphere. It just seemed that the more pressure the right-wingers put on the beleaguered president, the more popular he became.

And in retrospect, why shouldn't this be so? Despite the best efforts of the press and Republicans to express consternation at their lack of ability to turn public opinion against the president, the truth is that any reasonably sane person couldn't help but support the president during his 'ordeal.'

The case against him was, after all, built on the flimsiest of legal pretenses. In the final analysis, the entire case for removing Clinton from office was based on his having lied about receiving a blowjob, for God's sakes. And the entire case was built by running roughshod over the Constitution, a fact of which most Americans were innately aware.

It's really not surprising then that most leftists and centrists rallied to the support of the president. It's not even surprising that a good number of Republicans were steamrolled into supporting Clinton by the time the spectacle had reached its climax, so to speak.

It's also not surprising, as a side note, that the Republican Party did not, and does not, worry about repercussions for their actions from the American people at the voting booth. They are not in the least bit worried about losing control of the House and Senate. Not because it's not likely to happen – but because it doesn't matter if it does happen. Nothing is going to change, regardless of the relative mix of 'Democrats' and 'Republicans.'

The rhetoric surrounding the various policies being implemented may change, and which aspects of the agenda are being pushed may vary somewhat, but the agenda as a whole remains the same. There may be some advantage to the state though in achieving or maintaining a Republican majority, as it allows Congress to claim a 'mandate from the people' to more openly implement a fascistic agenda.

But the point here is that the impeachment was enormously successful in forcing the vast majority of Americans into fiercely supporting their president. And what did the administration proceed to do immediately after the impeachment came to a close with this unprecedented newfound popularity? Why, launch an unprovoked war on the nation of Serbia, of course.

This decidedly non-humanitarian military venture could have expected to meet with very vocal opposition from the American 'left' under ordinary circumstances. These were no ordinary circumstances, however. For well over a year leading up to the dropping of the first cluster bombs, the people had been herded like cattle into the president's corner.

We had expressed our collective wish that our president not be taken away from us. And throughout the entire sordid ordeal, we had the ever-present poll numbers to assure us that the majority of the country was on our side. Why, if you could stomach watching the cable news networks' twenty-four-hour Monicathons, you could practically track on an hourly basis the mood of the country concerning the impeachment throughout its myriad twists and turns.

Now flush with success from having successfully beat back the forces of the far-right, we were suddenly blind-sided by the outbreak of war. And what were we to do? And what did the rest of the country think about this development? Alas, there was no way to tell. Suddenly all the pollsters had disappeared, and there was nary a poll result to be found.

After an entire year of non-stop polling, the pollsters apparently needed a break. So we were left all alone to ponder what our fellow Americans felt about this foray into aerial warfare. And we couldn't very well abandon our president at that point, could we? He was still weak from his ordeal and needed our continued support.

And so it came to pass that the air war over Yugoslavia became known as a 'progressive war.' The left, who really should have known better, continued to support their president, and the right-wingers, who have never met a war they didn't like, rather preposterously continued to pose as opponents of Clinton and his policies.

This wasn't quite the last act in the play, however. There was still the matter of the congressional vote on the arms limitation treaty that followed the war for Kosovo. The truth of the matter is that neither side of the congressional aisle had the slightest intention of passing this measure *before* the supposed divisions brought about by the impeachment.

America's record on signing such agreements makes abundantly clear that the non-passage of this initiative was part of an historical pattern,[27] not the result of residual ill-will left over from the bitter impeachment battle. Nevertheless, the press dutifully reported to us that the measure had gone down to defeat as a direct result of the impeachment. It was, we were assured, a 'second vote' on the impeachment articles.

The press were well aware even as they reported this that it was a patently absurd notion. The animosities allegedly engendered by the impeachment were merely used as a convenient excuse for failing to pass an international treaty that never really had any chance of passing. It was just the latest act in the choreographed reality that comprises the American political system.

Besides solidifying Clinton's support as a prelude to launching a war and allowing the scapegoating of Congress' failure to pass an important international arms agreement, there are yet other purposes served by the impeachment of Clinton. One of these, perhaps not readily apparent, is that the proceedings served to exonerate him.

I am not referring here to the outcome of the vote on the impeachment articles in the Senate. That was a foregone conclusion. Even if one insists on retaining the belief that there are competing political parties in Washington, the mid-term removal of Clinton would have made no sense. Doing so would have allowed Al Gore to assume the presidency and to then run as an incumbent

---

[27] See *Derailing Democracy,* chapters 1 and 2.

president in the current election, greatly boosting his chances for victory.

But on a much broader scale, the entire nature and scope of the impeachment proceedings left an overwhelmingly positive portrait of William Jefferson Clinton. Consider, if you will, the vast array of charges, rumors, and innuendo surrounding this administration from its inception. Besides the rather frivolous—though numerous— allegations of sexual infidelities, Clinton had been accused of every- thing from drug trafficking and money laundering to murder.

There had been so many scandals hinted at during Clinton's first term that it was difficult to keep count. There was Whitewater, Filegate, Travelgate, and the Vince Foster case, among others. Although he was never explicitly cleared of any of these allegations, the implicit message was abundantly clear.

After all, didn't the impeachment zealots send the most rabidly anti-Clinton puritan it could find in search of dirt on the presi- dent? And didn't he and his equally determined band of merry men spend countless thousands of hours and millions of dollars in their single-minded quest to find any evidence that could topple mighty Bill?

Didn't they comb through every aspect of Clinton's life, both in Washington and Arkansas, bending and breaking the law as they saw fit? Were they not so determined to bring their man down that they were willing to do absolutely anything for any scrap of evidence to advance their cause?

And yet, in the final analysis, when everything was said and done, all they could find to hang on their prey was a charge of lying about a blowjob. They had looked under every rock, brow- beat every witness, searched through every swamp in Arkansas, and the worst that they could say about this scandal-plagued pres- ident was that he had tried to cover up an extramarital affair.

Well hot damn, forget about the impeachment – lets roll out the red carpet and crown the guy 'King for Life.' We just found the most honest politician in America! It's no wonder then that the proceedings served to vastly increase the support of the president among the people.[28]

Gone forever were those bothersome rumors. No longer would any credibility be given to spurious allegations about Whitewater, Filegate or Travelgate. Why, if Ken Starr couldn't find anything, there is obviously nothing there to find. Case closed.

If only that were true. Unfortunately, there is very definitely evidence, as previously cited, to suggest that Clinton was indeed involved in drug trafficking. And there is every reason to believe that the Whitewater affair was indeed a money laundering scheme to clean up some of the drug profits from those operations. And there is absolutely no chance that Ken Starr was unaware of this evidence.

But Bill has been cleared of any wrongdoing now, and so, not coincidentally, has his business partner George Bush – and by extension, his son George, Jr.. Also largely cleared by the proceedings was an alleged co-conspirator in various scandals, Vice President Al Gore. It really wouldn't do to have any of this type of baggage being carried by the chosen sons of their respective parties.

There is yet another purpose served by staging such an elaborate spectacle as was the Bill and Monica Show. To understand what that purpose was, it is important to understand that the pol-

---

[28] Even the notorious Starr Report, strangely enough, paints a positive portrait of the president. Despite the media fascination with the supposedly explicit sexuality, an objective reading of the document reveals a man tirelessly putting in inhumanly long hours at the service of his country. It also reveals a man in a position of great power who nevertheless has a rather pathetic sex life.

itics of illusion requires that any good politician must learn from the tradecraft of another type of performer – the stage magician.

As any good magician will tell you, the essence of magic is distraction and misdirection. The secret to performing a trick well is to succeed in getting the audience to watch your right hand when the trick is actually being performed with the left. And so it is with the performance of politics.

In this particular case, the at-times lurid impeachment marathon was the magician's right hand, and we stared at it mesmerized as though we were watching the trial of a wealthy black man accused of murdering a white woman. And all the while, that old left hand was robbing us blind.

Even as the press told us repeatedly that government was at a standstill until this matter was resolved (go ahead and keep staring at the right hand – you're not missing anything), Congress was indeed hard at work outside of the media spotlights, drafting and passing legislation that has dramatically more impact on your life than does the president's sex life. Really.

One final note on the subject of the impeachment, and a sobering one at that. The proceedings could have had another hidden purpose as well. The entire process could possibly have been intended as a test – a test of exactly how much undemocratic shenanigans the American people are willing to stomach before taking action.

By 'action' here, I mean something a little more profound than simply telling pollsters that they don't approve of the continuation of the proceedings. Something more along the lines of marching on Washington and demanding that the proceedings be halted and the undemocratic machinations exposed. Needless to say, if this was a test of that sort, we failed miserably.

Chapter 6

Fascism Reconstructed

For us there are two sorts of people in the world: there are those who are Christians and support free enterprise and there are the others.
Secretary of State John Foster Dulles

The purpose of the three preceding chapters has been to show that America is indeed a one-party state. To briefly recap, it has been argued that the notion of a multi-party state, or at least a two-party state, is a carefully crafted illusion and that virtually all politicians of any stature, particularly at the national level, are actors in this ongoing stage play who are well aware of the rules of the game.

It has been further argued that seemingly contentious political campaigns, far from being the winner-take-all slugfests that they appear to be, are intricately stage-managed acts in this grand illusion. Finally, it was suggested that the impeachment of President Clinton was not, in fact, indicative of deep divisions on Capitol Hill, but was rather yet another example of how the politics of illusion serves to bolster the false notion of competing ideologies in Washington.

Based on these arguments, I would suggest that America meets the criteria of being a one-party state. However, this is not the precise criteria we were trying to meet. It will be recalled that the component of the *Webster's* definition of *fascism* that was being explored was that of a *rigid one-party dictatorship.*

And a dictatorship is a different animal altogether. Or is it? I would contend that the only real difference between a one-party state and a one-party dictatorship is one of image. It is a difference in appearance, but not in function. In the American one-party state, the underlying structure and agenda of the government does not change, only the faces of the salesmen.

And the face of the head salesman at any given time is largely irrelevant. Such was the case as well in Nazi Germany. Contrary to conventional wisdom, Adolf Hitler was not an essential element of the fascist state. True, it always helps to have a charismatic front-man to sell the system, but there's always another waiting in the wings to take the reins.

In fact, there was a coup attempt made in Germany in 1944—shortly before the end of the war—the goal of which was to remove Hitler from power by assassination and replace him with Heinrich Himmler, while leaving the Nazi infrastructure intact. Had the attempt on Hitler's life succeeded, the strategy was to then seek a negotiated peace, allowing the kinder, gentler Germany to retain much of its plundered holdings.

The goal was, in other words, to change the face of fascism without changing the underlying structure, which is exactly what we do every four years when we hold another sham presidential election. And I might add that the transparency of the changing of the faces has been rather pronounced for the last twenty years or so.

Does anyone really believe that Ronald Reagan was actually steering the ship of state during his tenure? Of course not. He was never intended to. Ronnie just provided a telegenic face and a home-spun charisma – and a way to get the otherwise unelectable George Bush into the White House, which would make it a lot easier for George to run things while Ronnie chatted with his astrologer and took naps.

As if to emphasize this point, it was reported shortly after Reagan and Bush took office that: "Partly in an effort to bring harmony to the Reagan high command, it has been decided that Vice President Bush will be placed in charge of *a new structure* for national security crisis management, according to senior presidential assistants. The assignment will amount to an unprecedented role for a vice president in modern times."[29]

Strangely enough, a crisis developed just eight days later when the president was shot by would-be assassin John Hinckley, Jr. on March 30, 1981. We know, however, that this tragic occurrence was the work of a 'lone nut,' and not part of any conspiracy to do away with Reagan after he had fulfilled his purpose of getting the 'Republicans' into the White House.

As Bob Woodward later wrote, "[CIA Director William] Casey had a complete check done in CIA files on John Hinckley. Aware that, nearly twenty years after the Kennedy assassination, questions lingered about the connections between Lee Harvey Oswald and the KGB, Casey wanted to make sure this time. But there was nothing."[30]

There seems to have been some very interesting connections to Hinckley that Casey overlooked, however.[31] Apparently the CIA—America's premier information gathering network—doesn't have access to the *Associated Press* wire service, because if they

[29] Martin Schram "White House Revamps Top Policy Roles: Bush to Head Crisis Management," *Washington Post*, March 22, 1981 (emphasis added)

[30] Bob Woodward *Veil: The Secret Wars of the CIA 1981-1987,* Pocket Books, 1987

[31] As did reporter Woodward, who also doesn't appear to realize that the lingering doubts about Oswald concern his connections to the CIA, not the KGB. This could, of course, be due to the fact that Woodward's job before he became a reporter was as a top-security briefer for the Office of Naval Intelligence (Mark Zepezauer *The CIA's Greatest Hits*, Odonian Press, 1994).

did, Casey would certainly have known the day after the shooting that:

"The family of the man charged with trying to assassinate President Reagan is acquainted with the family of Vice President George Bush and had made large contributions to his political campaign ... Scott Hinckley, brother of John W. Hinckley, Jr. who allegedly shot at Reagan, was to have dined tonight in Denver at the home of Neil Bush, one of the Vice President's sons ... The Houston Post said it was unable to reach Scott Hinckley, vice president of his father's Denver-based firm, Vanderbilt Energy Corp., for comment. Neil Bush lives in Denver, where he works for Standard Oil Co. of Indiana. In 1978, Neil Bush served as campaign manager for his brother, George W. Bush, the Vice President's eldest son, who made an unsuccessful bid for Congress. Neil lived in Lubbock, Texas, throughout much of 1978, where John Hinckley lived from 1974 through 1980."[32]

All of which seems just a tad bit suspicious, but not enough so for the press to bother to run the story or for anyone in any branch of the federal government to feel the need to conduct any sort of inquiry into the unseemly connections between the vice president and the president's attempted assassin (astute readers will note that this is the third issue which will not be used against George W. Bush in his current presidential campaign, despite the fact that George, Jr. acknowledged to a reporter at the time that

---

[32] *Associated Press*, March 31, 1981

"It's certainly conceivable that I met him [John Hinckley, Jr.] or might have been introduced to him.").

This could of course all be entirely coincidental. In truth, Bush ultimately benefited by Reagan's having survived the attack, as this allowed him two terms of covert control of the White House prior to making his own run. And it's likely that Reagan had gotten the message loud and clear that he wasn't actually going to be running the show.

At any rate, after eight years of busying himself with the tedious details of running a ridiculously corrupt government—and being chided the entire time by the press for being a do-nothing vice president—George was ready to step out from the shadows and rule in his own right.

Of course, first he had to take care of that pesky Gary Hart guy, and then he had to toss the aforementioned Willie Horton at Michael Dukakis. But after all of that was over, the American people decided to give George a shot at running the country without wearing the Ronnie mask.

Unfortunately, four years later America decided it was time to change course, to bring in an entirely new administration. We didn't understand that the game can't be played that way. We're only allowed to change the face. So a nice 'Democratic' face named Bill Clinton was provided for us, and we obligingly pasted it over the same fundamentally corrupt political infrastructure.

So now we are once again in an election year, and it is time for George Bush's old crony Bill Clinton to go. And who shall his replacement be? If the country is in a Democratic mood, it has been ordained that it shall be Bill's ideological son, Al Gore. And should the conservatives prevail, it will be none other than George Bush's biological son, George, Jr.. And the song, either way, will remain the same.

If we accept then that America is a one-party state, and that a one-party state is equivalent in form and function to a one-party dictatorship, then we've now checked off five of the original six components of our definition. We're on the home stretch now. All that is left is the notion of *forcible suppression of opposition*.

To be fair, what we have in America is not so much *forcible* suppression of opposition as it is *structural* suppression of opposition. The system is not built, quite frankly, to allow for opposition. Opposition, that is, that falls outside of the 'two' major parties, unless one insists on counting the Reform Party as legitimate opposition.

A quick look at some of the Reform Party's potential candidates doesn't seem to include many reformers, however. It doesn't seem likely, for instance, that billionaire Donald Trump would seek to liberalize the agenda, so to speak. And the party's chosen candidate to lead the charge to the White House is probably the most openly fascistic politician in America today.

The fact that Pat Buchanan is even given legitimacy as a political candidate, largely due to the fact that he is given a high-profile media venue to legitimize his unsavory views, speaks volumes about the state of 'democracy' in this country. But the point is that if Buchanan were to prevail as the Reform Party candidate, about the only reform we would get would be to allow some of the covertly fascist infrastructure of the country to emerge from the shadows.

The Reform Party is, in other words, some type of hideous mutation spawned from the same primordial swamp from which emerged the American 'two-party' system. It was born from the realization by our wise leaders that Americans were beginning to have trouble remembering what the difference was supposed to be between Republicans and Democrats.

The facade was beginning to crack, and the American people in increasing numbers were looking for an alternative. And so was born a party to appeal to the reform-minded citizenry. Of course, there had been alternative parties around for decades, such as the Green Party and the Peace and Freedom Party; they had just never attained national stature virtually overnight.

Maybe that's because they tended to promote an actual agenda of reform. Maybe it's because they weren't led by a man with an ego and a bank account both much too large for any one man.[33] And maybe it's because they couldn't rely on saturation coverage and the conveyance of instant legitimacy by a corporate controlled media.

The truth of the matter is that the system is not designed to allow for upstart third parties. It can adjust to accommodate a patently bogus third party, and it can tolerate the occasional Republican or Democrat bolting his party to pose as an 'Independent,' but a real third party doesn't stand a chance.

That is why you won't find anything but Republicans and Democrats in the White House and the US Senate. Even the House of Representatives, reputedly the branch of the federal government most responsive to the people, counts just one Independent among its 435 members.[34]

---

[33] It should also be noted that H. Ross Perot had ties to the Central Intelligence Agency extending back at least fifteen years prior to his emergence on the national political scene as an 'outsider,' including the financing of some of Lt. Col. Oliver North's nefarious operations (Gordon Thomas *Journey Into Madness*, Bantam Books, 1989). Also notable is that Perot's company, EDS - the source of his considerable wealth - created computer surveillance systems for tracking immigrants and others of interest. For more on computer surveillance and tracking systems, see *Derailing Democracy*, chapters 15 and 22.

[34] The sole Independent, Bernie Sanders, is allegedly a Socialist, though his voting record hardly supports that notion. Some of his top aides jumped ship recently when his support for the bombing of Serbia and Kosovo revealed the fraudulent nature of his party affiliation.

That's because we all know that voting for a third-party candidate is just throwing your vote away. Which is, sadly, quite true. True because the American system of 'democracy' is a winner-take-all system. And a minor party candidate, lacking funding and media support, has exactly *no* chance of winning.

If, however, America were based on a representational system, as are the European democracies, winning would be a relative concept, and third-party votes would not be thrown away. For in that type of system, congressional or parliamentary seats are awarded proportionally based on the election outcome.

In other words, your party need not 'win' to gain representation. Every vote for your party gains greater representation, and no votes are thrown away. It is easy to see how this type of democracy could quickly erode the entrenched 'two-party' system.

Imagine not having to cringe as you force yourself to vote for one of the chosen sons so as not to 'throw your vote away.' And imagine how many other former Republicans and Democrats would choose to do likewise as they saw that their votes really did make a difference.

But don't spend too much time imagining it, because it's not going to happen. The structural obstacles to third parties will remain because that's the way the much-vaunted 'Founding Fathers' intended it to be. Otherwise, they would have given us a real democracy.

What they gave us instead is a system with structural suppression of legitimate opposition. And structural suppression, I would argue, is a veiled form of forcible suppression. Or to put it another way, structural suppression for the most part precludes the necessity of using overt force to suppress opposition.

Sometimes structural opposition alone is not enough, however. As anyone who attended the recent protests in Seattle, Philadelphia, or Los Angeles can readily attest, forcible suppression *will* be utilized if the level of dissent is seen as posing a potential threat to the system. This is certainly not a recent development.

Some of the more egregious uses of force to suppress dissent in this century include the killing of thirty-three striking mine workers by soldiers at the Rockefeller-owned Colorado Fuel and Iron Company in Ludlow, Colorado on April 20, 1914, and the killing of thirty-four African-American protestors and the wounding of a thousand more by US Army troops during an uprising in Detroit, Michigan on April 20, 1943. This occurred at precisely the time that tens of thousands of African Americans were deployed overseas, allegedly fighting to free Europe from just this type of fascist tyranny.

Assuming though that structural suppression is the preferred means for controlling dissent, we need merely to make a couple of minor modifications to our working definition of fascism—substituting the word *state* for the word *dictator,* and the word *structural* for the word *forcible*—to end up with: *a system of government characterized by a rigid one-party state, structural suppression of opposition, private economic enterprise under centralized government control, belligerent nationalism, racism, and militarism, etc.*

And there you have it – the American system of government in a nutshell. But wait, you say. How could we possibly be a fascist state? Aren't we the ones who selflessly sent our troops to distant lands during World War II to rid the world of the menace of European and Asian fascism? And did we not succeed in our quest?

Chapter 7

World War II, Through the Looking Glass

Once lead people into war, and they'll forget there ever was such a thing as tolerance. To fight you must be brutal and ruthless, and the spirit of ruthless brutality will enter into every fiber of our national life, infecting Congress, the courts, the policemen on the beat, the man in the street.
Frank L. Cobb of the New York World, 1917

World War II is much like any other significant event in US history in that it is cloaked in mythology. It is unlike other historical events though, in that even those who condemn virtually all other past uses of US military power tend to romanticize this particular war as a shining example of America 'doing the right thing.'

Our schools and our media—both news and entertainment—paint a picture of a heroic America saving the day by altruistically coming to the aid of an embattled Europe. But how much of this is historical truth and how much is historical revisionism? Much of what we 'know' about World War II, it turns out, falls into the latter category.

The purpose of this chapter, then, will be to examine some of the major myths surrounding WWII that have come to be almost universally accepted as historical facts. We shall begin with one of the more fanciful notions about the war:

Myth #1: Some European nations, despite being surrounded by combatants, managed to remain neutral throughout the war.

Sweden and Switzerland are almost universally believed to be two such nations. In truth though, both of these countries performed services vital to the Third Reich throughout the war, a fact that was well known to US officials – who nevertheless allowed the illusion of neutrality to stand, and continue to this day to do so.

Swiss banks handled much of the Reich's sordid financial affairs, as has been fairly widely reported.[35] Much of the gold looted by Germany, including tons of dental gold scavenged from the corpses of concentration camp inmates, was laundered through an intricate network of Swiss bank accounts. To this day, the banks have resisted paying compensation for their complicity in these crimes against humanity.

Less well known is the key role played by Sweden in keeping the German war machine in operation. One thing that a modern mechanized army needed to run was a steady supply of ball-bearings. Without them, planes would not fly, jeeps and tanks would not run, and artillery pieces would not operate.

Luckily for the Nazi regime, it had a rather cozy relationship with SKF, the Swedish ball-bearing trust that was in part an arm of the Swedish government.[36] SKF was the world's largest

---

[35] See, for example, John Loftus and Mark Aarons' *Unholy Trinity: The Vatican, The Nazis, and The Swiss Banks*, St. Martin's Press, 1998, and *A&E Investigative Reports* "Blood Money: Switzerland's Nazi Gold."

[36] All the information presented here on SKF is from Charles Higham's *Trading With the Enemy*.

manufacturer of ball-bearings, controlling 80% of the European market alone. During the war, fully 60% of SKF's total worldwide output was dedicated to the needs of the Reich.

This is not really surprising, given the cast of characters involved. The SKF story, though just one piece of a much larger puzzle, provides a good glimpse of the degree of collusion that existed between US and German industrialists and financiers during World War II.

One of the directors of SKF was Hugo van Rosen, a cousin of *Luftwaffe* chief Hermann Goering. Another was William L. Batt, who was also the president of American Bosch, a subsidiary of the I.G. Farben cartel. Both of these entities, along with a variety of other Nazi front companies, were represented and protected by John Foster Dulles of Wall Street's Sullivan & Cromwell.

In spite of (or perhaps because of) Batt's extensive connections to the Nazi cartels, he was appointed vice chairman of the War Productions Board by President Roosevelt. Batt was also an associate of Bush business partner Averell Harriman. At the end of the war, he popped up in Germany to pay a visit to the military 'decartelization' branch in Berlin.

The chief financier of SKF was Sweden's *Enskilda* Bank, a correspondent bank of Germany's *Reichsbank*. A major investor in the *Enskilda* Bank was 'Colonel' Sosthenes Behn, head of ITT – a longtime US intelligence front. ITT supplied the Reich with invaluable communications and missile guidance technology throughout the war.

And on and on the connections go. The main point here, though, is that Sweden was far from being a neutral bystander during the war. The country's corporate and financial infrastructure was actively and aggressively pro-Nazi, as was the case in

Switzerland as well. This was not only known to the heads of corporate America, it was wholeheartedly encouraged.

Myth #2: The Axis forces had not originally planned to invade the USSR. Hitler made the decision on something of a whim, believing that Russia could be quickly overrun, after which the westward push would resume. This proved to be a strategically unsound decision, requiring Hitler to redirect his forces to the Eastern Front.

This notion is completely unsupported by the historical facts. Every indication is that the Soviet Union was the primary target of the Axis European powers from the outset of the war. In fact, virtually every action taken by Germany's military forces prior to attacking the USSR was intended to gain strategic advantage to facilitate the attack on the ultimate target – the Soviet Union.

The initial problem for Germany was that they had no front on which to attack the great Red menace. There happened to be a number of other nations in the way, including, from north to south: Norway, Finland, the Baltic states of Estonia, Latvia, and Lithuania, Poland, Czechoslovakia, Hungary, Romania, and Bulgaria.

The most direct path to the Soviet Union's western frontier was through Poland and Czechoslovakia. Notably, these were the first nations to be plundered by the Reich—in March and September of 1939—following the voluntary annexation of Austria in March of 1938.

Modern accounts of the war tell us that the brutal assault on Poland was a joint venture of Germany and the USSR, planned and coordinated in advance. At the time, however, the Soviets heatedly denied these reports—which were issued from Berlin—as

Nazi propaganda, and contemporary Western news reports seconded that notion.[37]

Soviet Premier Josef Stalin maintained that he was not informed
of the planned invasion and that Soviet troops were sent in as a
defensive measure to stop the Nazi advance and secure a buffer
zone on the Soviet western frontier, which is indeed what appears
to have occurred.

The German troops entered Poland on September 1 with
blitzkrieg force, cutting a wide path of destruction across western
Poland. The Soviet troops did not enter until September 17, and
thereafter advanced quickly across the eastern half of Poland,
meeting the German troops midway just two days later.

In other words, the Soviets encountered little resistance and
covered nearly the same amount of ground in two days that the
Germans covered in nineteen, which could well indicate that the
Red Army entered in defense of Poland. It could also indicate simply that the vast majority of Poland's forces were deployed in the
west, and there was nobody left to resist the Soviet advance.

What is not in doubt is that Germany now had the beginnings
of a front with the USSR. Also not in doubt is that news accounts
at the time told of tens of thousands of Poles fleeing the German-
occupied zone into the relative safety of the Soviet-occupied zone
to escape the massive repression and bloodshed inflicted by the
Nazis.

---

[37] The information on World War II contained in this and the next chapter
is drawn from two very contradictory sources: modern mainstream accounts of
the war, including those of the *Encyclopaedia Britannica* and *Microsoft's
Encarta Encyclopedia,* as well as Norman Davies' *Europe* (Oxford University
Press, 1996); and a fascinating three volume account of the war that was written *as the events occurred* - Herman C. Morris and Harry B. Henderson's
World War II in Pictures (*Volumes I and II,* Doubleday, Doran & Company,
1942; and *Volume III,* The Greystone Press, 1946). The casualty figures used
throughout this chapter and the next come from the two encyclopedias and
from Davies' *Europe,* Appendix III.

The Soviets by this time, no doubt, knew exactly what the long-term German goal was, so they immediately set out to buffer their northwestern front. Less than a month after entering Poland, the Soviets occupied the Baltics and began negotiations with Finland, aimed primarily at buffering the city of Stalingrad, which lay within easy artillery range of the Finnish border.

When these talks broke down, the Soviets invaded, ultimately forcing an armistice which ceded them what they wanted. The Soviets were widely and loudly denounced for these actions—and even expelled from the League of Nations—though they insisted that the only actions taken were those necessary for the defense of the USSR.

The Soviet Union, it should be noted here, had already seen the original version of this film—called World War I—and so had a pretty good idea of what the script called for.[38] There is every reason to believe that they knew exactly what was coming. And they didn't have to wait long.

---

[38] World War I began on July 28 of 1914 allegedly as a regional conflict between Serbia and Austria/Hungary. Germany quickly entered the war on August 1, declaring war on, of course, Russia. The vast bulk of the fighting occurred on this front throughout the war, while the Western Front remained stationary for virtually the entire war. Trench warfare was the order of the day, with both sides dug-in and separated by a 'no mans land.' While casualties were high, no ground was gained by either side. As it would in World War II, the United States sat out much of the war. Congress did not declare war until April 6, 1917, and American troops did not see action in force until April of 1918. The war would be over before year's end, with the armistice being signed on November 11. In the end, Russian casualties - including dead, wounded, captured, and missing - totaled 9,150,000. American casualties numbered 350,300. Though it is frequently said that the first world war accomplished nothing, that is decidedly not the case. The war shattered three great empires: the Ottoman Empire in the Middle East, the Austro-Hungarian monarchy, and Czarist Russia. The result was that these war-torn areas were left destabilized and vulnerable to the machinations that would give rise to fascist rule.

Six months later, in April of 1940, Germany invaded Norway by way of Denmark, though neither really put up much of a fight. It was pretty much over before it even began, as was the occupation the very next month of the Netherlands and Belgium.

Next to fall was France—in June of 1940—which provided Germany with valuable strategic assets, including France's formidable armaments and entire Atlantic coastline. And it didn't require much of a fight either. Paris, for instance, was declared an 'open city' and fell without a fight at all, the first European capital to do so.

By November of 1940, Hungary and Romania had been occupied as well, extending the Russo/German Front to the south of Poland. In Romania, however, as in Poland, Soviet forces rolled in to cut off the Axis troops, seizing strategically valuable oilfields and cutting off direct access to Bulgaria.

The Germans nonetheless proceeded to plunder forth into Bulgaria by way of Yugoslavia and Greece, and by February of 1941, Bulgaria was an occupied nation, followed quickly by Yugoslavia in April and Greece in May. The Third Reich now had a solid Eastern Front and a stable rear extending all the way from Norway in the north to Bulgaria in the south.

The very next month, on June 22, 1941, the Germans attacked along this entire 1,800 mile front with the largest military mobilization of manpower in history – three million troops. The Germans were joined in the north by Finnish troops, in the south by Romanian troops, and along the center by Hungarian troops. Also joining in would be large contingents of Italian and Spanish troops. It was hardly an action taken on a whim.

For the next three years, virtually all the fighting in Europe was on the Eastern Front. The only offensive action taken by the Axis powers in Western Europe for the duration of the war was the bombing of England (to be discussed later). The US, of course, had yet to enter the war, though over a dozen formerly sovereign nations had been occupied.

The US continued to remain disinterested through the summer and fall as Nazi troops plundered deep into Soviet territory. They took notice only on December 6/7, 1941. December 6, it will be recalled, was the day the Soviets did something they weren't supposed to do – rallied a massive counterattack that began to push the German forces back.

And December 7, as everyone knows, was the morning that Pearl Harbor was bombed, bringing America quickly into the war. Which brings us to the next myth about WWII:

Myth #3: The bombing of Pearl Harbor was a surprise attack.

A number of researchers and historians over the years have presented evidence indicating that the US was aware of the impending attack and chose to feign shock and surprise, in order to lead a reluctant citizenry into what was, at the time, an unpopular war.[39]

Prior to the unexpected Soviet counteroffensive, a fierce battle had been waged to steer public opinion away from supporting US entry into the war. This effort was led by such notables as Charles Lindbergh, Father Coughlin, and Henry Ford, and organizations such as America First. The net result was that a major event was required to swing the pendulum of public opinion in the other direction – and quickly.

---

[39] See, most recently, *Day of Deceit* and Michael Zezima's *Saving Private Power*, Soft Skull Press, 2000

The timing of the attack then, is suggestive not just of US awareness, but quite likely of US complicity. In any event, the sequence of events leading up to, and on the day of, the attack certainly doesn't suggest that it came as much of a surprise. From a mainstream account written at the time[40], here is what occurred:

Late August, 1941 – Kichisaburo Nomura was dispatched to Washington to begin US/Japanese talks.

September 21 – The talks reportedly reached a deadlock.

November 15 – Talks resumed with negotiator Saburo Kurusu having been added to the Japanese team.

December 3 – Negotiations again reportedly reached a deadlock.

December 7 – Kurusu and Nomura resumed talks with US Secretary of State Cordell Hull in Washington. Meanwhile, at Pearl Harbor, Hawaii, a US Navy supply ship spotted a Japanese sub at 6:30 AM and ordered an air-strike on the location, but the crew did not sound an alarm. At 7:02 AM, Corporal Joseph Lockard—manning Pearl Harbor's aircraft detection system— spotted a large fleet of Japanese aircraft just 130 miles northeast of Oahu. His superiors inexplicably dismissed the fleet as US planes.

At 7:45 AM, another Japanese sub was spotted, this one having penetrated the submarine nets protecting the base. There was no US response. Ten minutes later, even as meetings were being held in Washington, the first bombs struck the naval base in a sus-

---

[40] *World War II in Pictures*

tained attack allegedly intended to disable the Pacific Fleet. Strangely though, shore installations and oil storage facilities were not targeted. And conveniently, all three US aircraft carriers—far and away the most valuable assets in the fleet—were out to sea.

Three-and-a-half hours after the initial attack, a second 'surprise' attack occurred at 11:29 AM, followed by another at 11:59 AM. These were followed by further 'surprise' attacks at 12:22 PM, 7:15 PM, and 9:10 PM, although—after awhile—the surprise factor must surely have been wearing a bit thin. Most of these later attacks seemed more concerned with bombing civilian centers and strafing the streets with machine-gun fire than with inflicting further damage on the naval base.

This obviously served no military purpose, but did serve to enrage the American people. In the end, the damage to the Pacific Fleet was relatively minimal. Six of eight battleships survived, along with—as previously noted—all three aircraft carriers and virtually all the shore installations vital to keeping the ships operational, leaving America very well-equipped to enter the war.

Myth #4: The United States entered the war primarily to check Nazi aggression in Europe. The parallel war in the Pacific was of secondary concern.

That's not quite the script that was followed. It is absolutely true that America entered the war with the *stated* goal of 'Europe First.' But in truth, despite repeated promises to Soviet leader Stalin to open a Western Front in Europe, it would be two-and-a-half years before this came to pass. In the meantime, the vast majority of US forces were deployed in the Pacific theater of operations.

With the exception of a ridiculously feeble attempt to establish a Southern Front in Italy in mid-1943—which proved to be of no strategic significance (though it was part of the covert game plan, as explained later)—American troops stayed away from Europe until D-Day, 1944. Meanwhile, Soviet troops fought for those same two-and-a-half years to halt the waves of Nazi invaders and reclaim their country.

These invaders included—in addition to the regular army troops of Germany and her allies—the so-called *Einsatzgruppen* and *Einsatzkommando* units, which were essentially mobile genocide squads. These units were activated in conjunction with the invasion of the Soviet Union, following behind the regular army forces to perform mass executions of anyone posing a 'threat' to the Reich. Following behind them were *Waffen SS* and *Gestapo* units, performing further acts of genocide. [41]

In opposition to this formidable killing machine, the Soviets stood largely alone. [42] And ultimately prevailed. By March 25, 1944, Soviet troops stood—for the first time in three years—on a portion of the pre-war border. By June, the entire Nazi Eastern Front was being pushed back and the defeat of Germany was inevitable; this is precisely when the US made its much heralded D-Day invasion of Normandy Beach on June 6.

Prior to this, as previously stated, America had been quite busy in the Pacific, conducting an island-hopping campaign to reclaim numerous island chains which had been occupied by fascist Japanese forces. Which brings up another myth:

Myth #5: Though the Axis powers conducted themselves in the most brutal and abominable fashion imaginable, America behaved admirably throughout the war.

---

[41] *A&E Investigative Reports* "The Nazis' Secret Killing Squads," April 21, 2000

[42] Davies writes in *Europe* that at the time of the Anglo-Soviet pact, 150 German divisions were deployed on the Soviet front, while only four divisions were assigned to the only other front, North Africa.

This is not, of course, a myth that is specific to this war. The enemy is always vilified and America is always portrayed as heroic, though this is rarely—if ever—the case. In World War II though, the 'enemies' did indeed conduct themselves in a most vile manner. But America was certainly a contender in the Atrocity Bowl as well.

Take, for example, the island of Iwo Jima, which is but a mere speck in the ocean with a total land area of just eight square miles. Prior to any troops being landed at Iwo Jima, it was bombed continuously for 72 days. Longer, that is, than the entire nation of Iraq in the 1991 Gulf War.

Following that, a naval force of several hundred ships and landing vessels was sent to encircle and shell the island around the clock for 72 hours, while bombers continued to drop napalm and explosives from above. Only then did troops set foot on Iwo Jima, to clear out any resistance burrowed into trenches and bunkers.[43]

To aid in this task, the US had introduced some new weaponry to its arsenal – hand-held and tank-mounted flame-throwers.[44] The intent was to literally burn the enemy alive in their fortified locations. And they worked great. Also brought in was the Marine War Dogs Division – canines specially trained to root out and attack the enemy.[45] In the end, only a hundred prisoners were taken alive on the entire island.

Any number of other islands were taken in a similar fashion. A war correspondent for the *Atlantic Monthly* gave readers a taste

[43] *World War II in Pictures.* As testament to the indomitable human spirit, resistance was met immediately.

[44] *World War II in Pictures.* It bears noting here that while this was a technique of warfare new to America, it was not new to the world's battlefields. Robin Lumsden notes in *Himmler's Black Order 1923-45* (Sutton, 1997) that flame-throwers had first been introduced by Germany in the latter part of World War I, where they were wielded by special 'death's head' regiments that would later evolve into Himmler's elite *SS.*

[45] *World War II in Pictures*

of the brutality of US forces in the Pacific Islands when he reported: "We shot prisoners in cold blood, wiped out hospitals, strafed lifeboats, killed or mistreated enemy civilians, finished off the enemy wounded, tossed the dying into a hole with the dead, and in the Pacific boiled the flesh off enemy skulls to make table ornaments for sweethearts, or carved their bones into letter openers."[46]

Time magazine later justified the brutal battle for Iwo Jima thusly: "The ordinary unreasoning Jap is ignorant. Perhaps he is human. Nothing .... indicates it."[47] In 1944, *Life* magazine ran a "full page photograph of an attractive blonde posing with a Japanese skull she had been sent by her fiancé in the Pacific."[48] *Time* also gleefully proclaimed that: "properly kindled, Japanese cities will burn like autumn leaves."[49]

That did, in fact, prove to be the case. In the final year of the war, Tokyo, Nagoya, Osaka, Kobe, Kure, Yokohama and sixty other so-called 'death-list' cities were carpet-bombed by US B-29 Superfortresses. The death toll was staggering. In Tokyo alone, as many as 85,000 Japanese lost their lives in a single night on March 9/10, 1945, when 1,665 tons of incendiary weapons were dropped.[50]

By the end of the war, over 40% of the surface area in the death-list cites had been destroyed. On July 3, 1945, Tokyo reported that nearly five million Japanese had been left dead, wounded, or homeless by the relentless bombing raids. General

---

[46] David E. Stannard *American Holocaust*, Oxford University Press, 1992
[47] Howard Zinn *A People's History of the United States*, Harper and Row, 1995
[48] *American Holocaust*
[49] *Saving Private Power*
[50] *Saving Private Power*

Curtis LeMay, who led the air campaign, acknowledged its savagery when he noted that: "I suppose if I had lost the war, I would have been tried as a war criminal."[51]

And, lest we forget, it was the United States that dropped the atomic bombs on Hiroshima and Nagasaki – on a country whose navy and air force were destroyed, and which was blockaded by sea and air and essentially defeated at the time. This brings up another myth about the war, which will be addressed after first noting that American brutality was certainly not confined to the Pacific theater.

US and British air power wreaked considerable havoc in Europe as well. While our modern accounts of the war emphasize the recurrent attacks on England by *Luftwaffe* bombers, the official casualty figures for the war turn up a rather curious anomaly. If these figures are to be believed, then about 60,000 civilians lost their lives in the UK throughout the course of the war. This is surely not an insignificant loss of life.

But consider that a single sustained incendiary bombing attack on the city of Dresden, Germany by the US and the UK left 130,000 dead.[52] In other words, twice as many German civilians were killed in a single city in just one weekend than were British civilians throughout all the years of the war. Another 50,000 were similarly incinerated in Hamburg, Germany. And so on.

This is not to say that the *Luftwaffe* didn't actively participate in the mass execution of civilians, or that German troops didn't

---

[51] *Saving Private Power*

[52] Dresden was, it should be noted, largely a community of artists and artisans, with very little industry and virtually no defense production. It was precisely the type of community, in other words, where one would anticipate finding the greatest *resistance* to the Nazi regime. Michael Parenti and others have noted that US pilots were given specific instructions not to bomb facilities in Germany in which American firms had investments.

commit the most heinous of war crimes. Most certainly they did, as did Japanese forces in the Pacific. But that certainly does not excuse America's behavior in the war, which was far from honorable.

Myth #6: The atomic bombing of Hiroshima and Nagasaki led directly to the Japanese surrender and thereby saved hundreds of thousands of lives.

There are in fact numerous interwoven myths that need to be addressed here. What is needed first, however, is a very brief review of the war in the Pacific that led up to the bombings, in order to provide some context for this seminal event in world history.

Japan fired the opening salvos of World War II when it invaded Manchuria in 1931, an area in which it had vast financial holdings. The US completely ignored this illegal act of aggression. From there, Japanese troops showed every intention of proceeding on into Soviet territory – until Red Army forces were mobilized at the border, prompting the Japanese forces to wisely reconsider.

By the next year, 1932, the US was sending 13,000 tons of scrap iron annually to Japanese munitions factories to craft explosives. Japan was, at the time, led by a 'secret' occult order dubbed the 'Society of the Black Dragon,' a not-so-secret fact at the time, though discussion of such topics today is considered to be 'conspiracy theorizing.'[53] The Society used assassination as a primary

---

[53] *World War II in Pictures* openly discusses the existence of the Society, as well as the scrap iron shipments. What isn't mentioned is that Germany was also largely run by a closely-knit group of 'secret societies,' including the *Thule Gesellschaft* and the *Germanenorden* (*Unholy Alliance*).

political tool, and controlled over 100 smaller organizations and the majority of the nation's politicians and military leaders.

By the next year, 1933, US shipments of scrap iron had increased more than ten-fold, to 142,000 tons. Hitler, meanwhile, took power in Germany and immediately began preparing the nation to attack the Soviet Union. In 1936, Germany and Japan signed the anti-Comintern treaty. In December of the following year, Japanese fighter planes attacked and sunk the US gunship Panay, and followed that up by machine-gunning the crew as they desperately struggled to get ashore in life rafts. The US essentially ignored the brutal attack.

In 1938, Japan was again engaging in border skirmishes with the USSR, and getting consistently crushed by the Red Army. By the following year, The US had increased its shipments of scrap iron to 607,000 tons, and was shipping high-octane aviation fuel as well, to assist with the delivery of the armaments it was helping to create.

Besides jousting with the Soviets, Japan was also attacking and occupying every other nation and island chain in sight. Along the way, it built a number of state-of-the-art military airfields, which would later be occupied and utilized by the US. These airfields would play a vital role in the fire-bombing of the death-list cities.

In September of 1940, the infamous Pact of Berlin was signed by Germany, Italy and Japan. Seven months later, Japan signed a neutrality agreement with the Soviets, mirroring the non-aggression pact offered to Stalin by the Nazis in August of 1939 – which had been a rather transparent effort by the fascist powers to falsely reassure the Soviets.

December of 1941, of course, saw America's entry into the war and the beginning of a long and bloody battle for control of the Pacific. By June of 1944, Japan had relinquished virtually all of its newly acquired territories to the US, and bombings of Japanese civilian centers began. In November, the bombings were stepped up dramatically.

August 6, 1945 marked the first offensive use of an atomic weapon as a uranium bomb was unleashed by the United States on the unsuspecting citizens of Hiroshima at 9:15 AM. 68,000 buildings and more than a hundred thousand men, women and children instantaneously ceased to exist.

Two days later, the USSR—which had agreed to stay out of the Pacific war for a period of ninety days following VE Day— declared war on Japan and entered Manchuria and Korea. On that same day, Soviet Foreign Commissar Molotov revealed that Tokyo had made a peace bid *before* the Potsdam Conference held the previous month.

The following day, a slightly different version of America's new weapon—a plutonium bomb—was dropped on Nagasaki, killing tens of thousands more Japanese civilians. Five days later, Japan surrendered, though fighting with the Soviets continued for another week, with the USSR seizing some 500,000 square miles of Manchuria as a buffer.

What then, through all of this, are we to make of the bombings? It seems fairly clear that the resort to atomic weaponry was not *necessary* to end the war. As previously noted, it was revealed several days before the bombing of Hiroshima that the US had successfully sown mines in all of Japan's ports, and that Japan's air force and navy were in shambles. The nation was, in other words, physically isolated and militarily disabled.

But did the bombings *hasten* the end of the war? This doesn't seem likely either. While the new weapon of war certainly wreaked massive destruction, the cities of Hiroshima and Nagasaki did not fare much worse, in the final analysis, than did any of the other death-list cities. America had already proven repeatedly that it could inflict appalling levels of property damage and rack-up mind-boggling body counts without resort to atomic bombs (of course, the atomic bombs would continue killing long after the war ended, but this was not well understood at the time).

The first bombing did not in fact bring an immediate surrender from the Japanese, though that is not likely the reason for the dropping of the second bomb.[54] It appears as though America wanted to compare the effectiveness of the two different weapons. And even the second bombing did not elicit an immediate response from Japan. The most likely reason for the surrender was the entry into the war of the Soviet Union, a fact acknowledged by more thoughtful historians, and one that was conceded in a top-secret US study conducted just a year after the war.[55]

As for the myth that the bombings saved countless lives, that is a blatantly absurd notion. Statements by President Truman and others over the years have put forth claims that as many as a million US lives were saved by avoiding an invasion of the Japanese mainland. Considering that this would represent nearly four times the number of American lives lost throughout the war, such claims appear rather specious.

In any event, any claims that promote the notion that deploying weaponry specifically designed to snuff out tens of thousands of lives somehow constitutes an effort to *save* lives are too ridiculous to merit comment. Returning then to the D-Day invasion of France: it is June of 1944, and the United States is finally opening up the long promised Western Front. Which brings us to the next myth:

---

[54] Both bombs, in fact, appear to have been dropped as a warning shot to the Soviet Union. They were, in a very real sense, the first offensive actions of the so-called Cold War. As Gore Vidal noted recently in an interview for the Prague Writers' Festival: "I don't think there was one single general officer in that war who approved of [dropping the atom bomb], and they all went public very quickly to denounce their Commander-in-Chief Truman, who had dropped it for one reason: to intimidate Stalin, keep him out of the Pacific war, let him have no share of the peace that we were going to impose on Japan" (*Guardian Unlimited*, March 29, 2001).

[55] *Saving Private Power*

Myth #7: The opening of the Western Front was the event that turned the tide of the war and played an essential role in the defeat of Nazi Germany.

Not quite. By D-Day it was abundantly clear that Germany was facing near imminent defeat with or without us. By July of 1944, with the Allies yet to break out of their secure beachhead to form the Western Front, the USSR had reclaimed all its pre-war borders and made clear that it wasn't going to stop there.

Having been subjected to two massive invasions from the West in the preceding twenty-five years, they fully intended to create a permanent buffer zone and to fully dismantle the German war machine. Already, they had begun penetrations into Poland and Lithuania.

This was precisely the time when the aforementioned coup attempt was made that would have replaced Hitler. Knowing that Germany could not stop the Red Army from rolling on through Eastern Europe, the goal was to seek a negotiated peace by pasting a new face on the fascist regime.

US intelligence services were fully complicit in this attempt to preserve the Reich. America's premier spymaster—Allen Dulles—working through his post as OSS chief in Bern, Switzerland, had brokered the deal with the Nazis. Dulles believed, correctly no doubt, that Western public opinion would not support a negotiated peace leaving Hitler in power.[56]

---

[56] Christopher Simpson *The Splendid Blond Beast,* Grove Press, 1993 and Martin Lee *The Beast Reawakens,* Routledge, 2000

At around this same time, Dulles was involved in other secret negotiations with the *SS,* dubbed Operation Sunrise, aimed at achieving a German surrender in northern Italy – which would have allowed the Allies to advance to the port city of Trieste. From there, Austria, Hungary and Yugoslavia could all have been quickly penetrated in advance of the Red Army.[57]

Had the coup proven successful, that could conceivably have ended the war before the Western Front was even formed, and with Eastern Europe securely in Axis hands. It's quite possible— indeed quite likely—that the USSR would have rejected this 'peace.' It is also possible that the Allies could have at that time joined with the Axis in waging war on the Soviets – who could have been painted as the aggressors for failing to accept the armistice.

But we will never know since the coup attempt failed, and five days later—on July 25—the Allies broke out from their beachhead and the fabled Western Front was born. The Red army was at that time less than 100 miles from Warsaw and pushing on. Fully eighty percent of Germany's troops were engaged on the Eastern Front.[58]

The war in Europe would be over in just nine months. From there on out, it became essentially a race for Berlin, a race that the Allies on the Western Front would ultimately lose. Interrupting their westward push somewhat, the Soviets also sent troops in to

---

[57] *The Splendid Blond Beast*
[58] *A People's History of the United States*

occupy and fortify the Baltics, Romania, Bulgaria, Yugoslavia, and Hungary.

The battle lines of the Cold War were being drawn – battle lines that would almost overnight see the United States and Britain embrace the European Axis powers of Italy and Germany as allies in opposition to their former ally in the east. Sound confusing? Not really. In truth, the Cold War battle lines weren't so very different from the battle lines of World War II, or of World War I for that matter. Which brings up the final myth:

Myth #8: World War II was primarily a war against European Jewry.

This is, alas, a most sensitive subject. There is always the danger of being labeled an anti-Semite, or worse yet, a Holocaust denier. I do not intend here, however, to cast any aspersions on the Jewish religion, or to deny—in any way—that some six million Jews were brutally murdered during World War II.

There is no doubt that that is indeed the case. But it is also the case that those six million deaths constituted only about ten percent, perhaps even less, of the total death toll directly attributable to WWII. And by focusing on those six million to the exclusion of the other sixty million lives lost, we blind ourselves to what the war was really about.

For what World War II really was, in the simplest possible terms, was a war against leftism – whether labeled as communism, socialism, or liberalism. In a broader sense, it was a war against the people: a war to exert the right of a relatively few powerful monopoly capitalists to oppress, exploit, and—if necessary—kill the people of the world for financial gain.

Thirteen-and-a-half million of those people killed were Chinese. And an astounding twenty-five million of them were Soviets. Another eight or nine million of them were Poles. Yet another five to eight million were German or Austrian. While it is true that many of those killed in Poland, Germany/Austria and the Soviet Union were Jewish, the vast majority of them were not.

And very few of those killed in China were likely of the Jewish faith. And yet we never talk of the Chinese Holocaust, to honor the memory of the millions slaughtered there. Nor is their any mention of the Russian Holocaust, or the Polish Holocaust.

Everyone, however, is aware of the Jewish Holocaust, or as we know it, *The* Holocaust. And it is this notion, the idea that the genocide of European Jews was an event unique to history, to which I object. In truth, it wasn't even an event unique to the war in which it occurred.

Genocide was the order of the day. But again, the primary targets were those on the political left, or at least those living in countries that adopted an overtly leftist political ideology. A good number of those people happened to be Jewish. But twice as many happened to be Chinese. And four times as many happened to be non-Jewish Russians.

This is not to suggest that Jews were targeted *only* for their political beliefs. There is no doubt that Jews were persecuted specifically as an ethnic group. But the point is that they were not the *primary* target, but a secondary one that fulfilled a need of the fascist state to identify false enemies (for reasons which will be explained in chapter 9).

The primary purpose of World War II was to wipe out any and all pockets of leftist resistance to the Reich's plans. Though that fact is difficult to discern from modern histories of the war, the officially accepted casualty figures tell a story all their own.

Chapter 8

World War II, By the Numbers

Fascism, which did not fear to call itself reactionary when many liberals were prone before the triumphant beast [Democracy], has not today any impediment against declaring itself illiberal and anti-liberal
Benito Mussolini, 1923

In the previous chapter it was shown how the belief that Jews were the primary victims of World War II is not supported by the raw numbers. In a war that caused at least forty million civilian deaths and sixty to seventy million total deaths, just six million of those were Jews.

This begs the question of why it is these six million that we remember. That is a question that must be addressed lest the reader infer that I'm suggesting some kind of Jewish conspiracy to garner unwarranted international sympathy. Not in the least.

What I am suggesting is a 'conspiracy' by Western capitalist interests not to garner sympathy for the Jews, but to deliberately misrepresent the conduct and the goals of World War II: to disguise a war that was very much a war between capitalism and socialism—or fascism and communism, if you prefer—as a war motivated by a desire for ethnic cleansing.

It should be noted though that there was a short-term goal that was served by generating international sympathy for the plight of European Jews: the creation of the nation of Israel in 1948. Though this was portrayed as a humanitarian act, the primary purpose was to set up a permanent military power (and a nuclear one at that) in the Middle East under the direct control of the West.

That this was the primary motivation is made clear by the fact that the two men who were most responsible for securing the necessary UN votes to recognize the state of Israel—John Foster Dulles and Nelson Rockefeller—were not exactly known for being sympathetic to the plight of the Jews during the war. Rockefeller's Standard Oil had, after all, been instrumental in keeping the Nazi war machine running smoothly.

Just as the belief that World War II was a war against European Jewry can be debunked by the casualty figures, so too can other myths about the war – such as the notion that the invasion of Russia was undertaken on something of a whim. If so, it was an incredibly bloody whim.

As previously stated, some twenty-five million Russians perished in the war, comprising about half of the roughly fifty million total deaths in Europe. And even this figure does not tell the full story. The vast majority of Germany's three to four million military casualties, as well as the 600,000 Romanian, Finnish, and Hungarian military casualties, died on the battlefields of Russia as well.

All told, as many as 2/3 of the total European casualties fell on Soviet and Polish soil, and an even larger majority of the casualties fell on the Eastern Front as a whole. The total casualties in Eastern Europe (including Bulgaria, Czechoslovakia, Greece, Hungary, Romania, Yugoslavia, Poland, the Soviet Union, and

Germany/Austria) throughout the course of the war was some-where around forty-five million.

The casualties among the Western European nations (Belgium, Denmark, France, the Netherlands, Norway, Finland, and Italy), on the other hand, totaled just one-and-a-half million, or about 3% of the estimated European total. Any notion then that the Eastern Front was of secondary significance to the Western Front is patently absurd.

Other rarely reported facts about the war also make clear that the West was of little concern to the war-planners of the Third Reich. After consolidating power in Western Europe fairly early in the war, the only offensive action taken by the Nazis was the bombing of England, allegedly as preparation for a full-scale inva-sion of the UK.

Though the occupation of the British Isles is claimed to have been a primary goal of the German war machine, this assertion is contradicted by the fact that the majority of German pilots shot down and captured over England were young and poorly trained, some still in their teens, and the aircraft they were flying tended to be among the older planes in the *Luftwaffe's* formidable arsenal of fighter craft.[59]

They were, in other words, disposable pilots flying disposable aircraft, while the cream of the German Air Force remained engaged on the Eastern Front. The same can be said of the land

---

[59] *World War II in Pictures*

forces sent by Germany to engage the Allies following the invasion at Normandy Beach.

The first division to resist the invasion was the *12th SS-Panzer Division Hitlerjugend*, a specially assembled 10,000 'man' cannon-fodder force composed entirely of seventeen-year-old 'Hitler Youth' volunteers, which by the end of the war was reduced to 455 men and a single tank.[60] The elite of Himmler's *SS* forces, needless to say, were much too busy in the east to be bothered with resisting the Yanks.

The truth, which should be glaringly obvious, is that World War II was—in the European theater—primarily a war against the Soviet Union. And in the Pacific it was primarily a war against China, which contributed thirteen-and-a-half million of the fifteen-and-a-half million total deaths attributed to that theater of operations.

It should be noted here that the total casualties listed for the Pacific theater are unnaturally low, in that only the figures for the three largest nations involved in the conflict are given: China, Japan, and the Philippines. Notably missing are casualty figures for the countless island chains that suffered through brutal attacks, first by the Japanese and later by the Americans and their allies.

As previously stated, these island-hopping campaigns involved a massive loss of life, an aspect of the war that is notably obscured by the omission of these casualty figures. Also notable in the

---

[60] *Himmler's Black Order 1923-45*

casualty figures given for Asia is the number of civilian deaths listed for Japan: 400,000. The unfortunate truth is that this number was quite likely surpassed just with the atomic bombings of Hiroshima and Nagasaki and the incendiary bombing of Tokyo.

But while the casualty figures don't reveal all of the truths about World War II, they do reveal many – such as the fact that the fighting in Europe was conducted overwhelmingly on the Eastern Front. Also revealed is that the Western European nations, by and large, offered only token resistance to the Nazi occupation, while several of the Eastern European countries waged fierce battles with their occupiers.

Denmark, for instance, suffered only 1,800 military casualties and Norway just 3,000. The Netherlands and Belgium suffered only slightly more, with 7,900 and 12,000 respectively. By contrast, Greece lost 88,000 men in uniform, Poland 123,000, and Yugoslavia 305,000. And the Soviet Union, the primary and at times sole defender of the Eastern Front, lost from eight to twelve *million* military personnel.

And how, you may ask, does this compare to the sacrifices made by the United States on the Western Front? You probably don't want to know. The *total* American military casualties through the duration of the war was 292,000.

Most of these casualties, it can be safely deduced, occurred in the Pacific, where the Americans began fighting two years before entering Europe and continued fighting for several months after the cessation of hostilities in Europe. Some of them died as well in Africa and the Middle East. And a few thousand of them died at a place called Pearl Harbor.

It's safe to assume then that maybe a third, *at most*, of American casualties were suffered on the belatedly opened Western Front. And what of the Brits, who entered the war a full two years before the US? They too lost less than 300,000 military men, also divided among the various theaters of operation.

It is said that over one million people lost their lives in the battle for Stalingrad, considered the largest single military battle in history.[61] As many lives lost in the defense of a *single* Soviet city than were lost by the soldiers and citizens of the United States, Great Britain and France combined through the *entire course* of the war.

Which nation was it then that almost single-handedly crushed the aspirations of the Third Reich? Who really won the war in Europe? Was it the couple of hundred thousand Yanks who gave their lives? Or was it the eight million or more Russians who gave theirs? The answer seems fairly clear.

One final note on the subject of World War II casualties: of all the countries invaded during the course of the war, one had the rather unique distinction of having far and away the lowest ratio of civilian to military deaths. This country, Finland, had only 2,000 civilian deaths compared to 82,000 military deaths.

No other country touched by the war had anywhere near such a ratio. In fact, in virtually all the Eastern and Western European countries, civilian casualties far *surpassed* military casualties. Only in Finland, it appears, was an effort made to avoid the targeting of civilians. And that was the action, it will be remembered, for which the Soviet Union was vilified.

---

[61] *Europe*

Chapter 9

Coming to Terms With the F-Word

In periods of acute crisis for the bourgeoisie, Fascism resorts to anti-capitalist phraseology, but, after it has established itself at the helm of state, it casts aside its anti-capitalist rattle, and discloses itself as a terrorist dictatorship of big capital. Fascism is the open terrorist dictatorship of the most reactionary, most chauvinist and most openly imperialist elements of finance capital.

Palme Dutt, 1933

The ugly truth is that the United States did not go to war in Europe in 1941 to stop the spread of European fascism. Rather, we entered the war to be sure that we got there in time to oversee the process of denazification. And in the US-occupied western half of Germany, and throughout the rest of Western Europe as well, that consisted largely of allowing the corporate, financial, and political infrastructure to remain.[62]

---

[62] See *The Beast Reawakens* and *The Splendid Blond Beast*

It also consisted of shielding from prosecution and exporting out of the country thousands of suspected war criminals. Some of the most appalling of these were sent to South America—with the blessings and assistance of US intelligence services—to engage in such activities as orchestrating coups, training death squads, trafficking in arms and drugs, and plotting assassinations.[63]

Others were recruited from throughout Eastern Europe for the purpose of organizing and leading rabidly pro-fascist émigré groups as propaganda tools of the Cold War.[64] Entire Nazi intelligence networks—including the infamous Gehlen Organization[65] and the commando unit of Otto Skorzeny[66]— were preserved relatively intact and incorporated into US intelligence services.

And then, of course, there were the Nazis brought here to America, most visibly the rocket team of Werner von Braun, credited with sending America to the moon. But this group was only the tip of the iceberg. Vast numbers of scientists, doctors, and academics were welcomed with open arms, regardless of their wartime records.[67]

They were placed in military facilities all across the country. They were actively recruited by US defense contractors and other corporate interests. Their expertise was utilized at Fort Detrick and the Edgewood Arsenal, homes of US biological and chemical warfare, respectively. And perhaps even more disturbingly, they were given professorships at universities around the country.

---

[63] See Ladislas Farago's *Aftermath,* Simon and Schuster, 1974, Peter Lavenda's *Unholy Alliance*, Avon, 1995, and Alexander Cockburn and Jeffrey St. Clair's *Whiteout*, Verso, 1998

[64] Christopher Simpson *Blowback*, Weidenfeld and Nicholson, 1988

[65] *Blowback;* Linda Hunt *Secret Agenda*, St. Martin's Press, 1991; Carl Oglesby "The Secret Treaty of Fort Hunt," *Covert Action Information Bulletin #35*, Fall 1990

[66] *Unholy Alliance* and *The Beast Reawakens*

[67] *Blowback, Secret Agenda*

It is fair to say then that far from containing and removing the cancer of fascism, we allowed it to spread, with the most tragic results occurring in Central and South America. But North America was infected as well, as fascism came home to roost in America's universities, corporations, military institutions, and communities.

But what of Japan? While it can reasonably be argued that the US did not enter the war in Europe in order to defeat Nazi Germany, but rather to preserve as many of the 'gains' made by the regime as possible, this argument surely does not apply to the situation in the Pacific. In stark contrast to the actions taken in Europe, America waged a prolonged, no-holds-barred war against Japan.

Why was Hitler's Asian partner treated so differently than was Germany itself? And why did Japan launch a bizarre and isolated attack on Pearl Harbor that was never followed up with any subsequent offensive actions, and which served only to draw America into the war – an entirely predictable result? And why did a regime organized on explicitly racist principals, preaching a doctrine of Aryan supremacy, welcome with open arms an Asian partner?

This final question, perhaps, provides the answers to the others. It is a rather remarkable fact that the sincerity of the German/Japanese alliance has never been seriously questioned, despite the rabid racism of the Nazi Party. It seems reasonable to conclude that the Japanese were used, unwittingly perhaps, by Germany (and her silent partners) to further Western aims.

Germany's acceptance of Japan was not likely a sincere gesture, but a cynical move to temporarily co-opt the nation's formidable military might to gain control over much of Asia. Hundreds of thousands of Japanese lives were lost doing the dirty work of 'pacifying' and occupying its neighbors, the benefits of which would later transfer to the West.

It seems inconceivable that Japan would have made the decision to attack Pearl Harbor on its own. Surely there had to be some prompting from the European fascist powers. Otherwise, the action makes absolutely no sense – other than as a moment of temporary insanity for Japan's otherwise highly successful military planners.

Dragging the US into the war was simply inexplicable, unless Japan was planning on making it an offensive war against the United States, which was clearly not the case. To deliberately set one's self up in a defensive posture against an immensely powerful foreign aggressor, with nothing to gain even in victory, makes sense only if Japan expected no more than a token attack by the US, as later occurred in Europe.

Was Japan in fact duped into ruthlessly pacifying the region, and then drawing the US into the war, inviting their own destruction? They certainly made it easy—relatively speaking, of course—for the US to gain control of their plundered holdings – having already wiped out much of the resistance, not to mention building all those airfields.

All of this, of course, is largely speculation. But isn't every telling of history, in the final analysis, speculation based on the bast available evidence? Unfortunately, the truth lies safely locked away in government vaults, so the best we can ever do is speculate based on what is known. And one thing that is known for sure is that, though we went to war in the Pacific to defeat a fascist power, it was only to replace its control with that of another fascist power.

This is not to say, however, that America's men and women in uniform did not go overseas with the intention and the belief that their mission was to eradicate the plague of fascism. Most assuredly they did, just as hundreds of thousands of men and women went off to serve in Vietnam and Korea thinking that they were fighting to stop the spread of 'international communism.'

But the justifications given to America's people—and to America's soldiers—for going off to war are rarely, if ever, the actual reasons for the United States' resort to military intervention. That's one of the problems with being an imperialist nation: when you routinely enter armed conflicts as an aggressor nation, you can't very well tell the people why they are being sent off to die.

So it really shouldn't surprise anyone to find that World War II was not the high-minded use of military force that it is nearly universally portrayed to be. Why should this war be any different than the rest? After all, the US has used its military might around the globe for this entire century for the purpose of deposing democratically minded governments and installing in their place overtly fascist military regimes.[68]

Of course, some will surely argue that it was not the *fascist* infrastructure that we preserved in Germany, but rather the *free market* infrastructure. By this reasoning, it was not the economic system which was a problem, just the rampant imperialism and genocide.

Essentially the same argument is made to justify US interventions in the Third World: it is only free market, 'democratic' reforms we are promoting. The severe repression, death squads,

---

[68] For the most complete chronology of American military actions since World War II, both overt and covert, see William Blum's *Killing Hope,* Common Courage Press, 1995. Blum provides extensive documentation of the anti-democratic goals pursued by the United States in literally dozens of nations around the world.

and occasional acts of genocide that accompany these 'reforms' are entirely unconnected and unforeseen events.

In other words, it's not the *private economic enterprise under centralized government control* to which we take offense, it's the *belligerent nationalism, racism, militarism, forcible suppression of opposition,* and *one-party dictatorship.* So it really doesn't matter that *Webster's* has removed that reference to free enterprise from the definition of the f-word; all that has been removed is an aspect of the system that is unconnected to the others and is the sole redeeming feature of the fascist state.

This would be a nice story were it not based on a completely false notion. The truth is that it is precisely the structure of private enterprise that defines the fascist state. For as no less an authority than Benito Mussolini defined it, "Fascism is corporatism." Corporate control of the state is, and always has been, the primary goal and agenda of the fascist state.

All of the other aspects of fascism—the belligerent nationalism, militarism, racism, etc.—are actually tools with which the state is kept propped up. And these tools are absolutely essential to maintain the system; without them, the corporate state could not survive for any length of time. The people, whose interests are subverted for the grossly disproportionate benefit of a few, would not allow the system to stand. That is why all 'Western democracies,' including the United States, display these unsavory aspects to varying degrees.

The degree to which these other aspects are manifest is directly proportional to the degree to which the market is allowed to function without restraint. Overt fascism is, in other words, capitalism in its purest form – monopoly corporate capitalism, such as is currently on display in America.

And the closer we get to unrestrained corporate power, the more overt will become the racism, militarism, etc. For these, as stated, are the tools used to legitimize the system. They fulfill the needs of the state to divide the populace and generate false enemies, both at home and abroad. For a people divided, a people at war with themselves, are not a threat to the state. And a people encouraged to scapegoat an ethnic group for the problems of society will fail to see that people of all ethnicities have a common enemy in the fascist state.

And so it was that the Jews became a convenient scapegoat for the misplaced anger and frustration of the German and Austrian people. And so it is that immigrants are now a convenient scapegoat for the American people, as are Blacks, Jews, gays and any other group that can be divided and set up as a warring camp.

By providing the people with a false target for their frustrations with the ills of society, racism plays an integral role in stabilizing the state by misdirecting the wrath of the people away from the true source of societal decay, the fundamentally corrupt and anti-democratic system that is corporate capitalism.

So too is the system stabilized by the elements of militarism and belligerent nationalism. False enemies abroad are just as important as false enemies at home, if not more so, for false enemies abroad serve at least one additional function beyond redirecting the anger of the people onto a blameless group – to justify the imperialist military interventions that are an essential feature of the corporate state.

For the corporate capitalist state, and therefore the fascist state, is inherently imperialistic. The unbridled greed for ever greater profits for the few fuels the need for conquest. New labor markets need to be oppressed and exploited, new resource markets need to be raped and pillaged, and new consumer markets need to be created. The fascist state cannot rest until it devours every available market.

So the wheels of globalization (the media friendly euphemism for global fascism) will continue to spin. Yet even as more and more of the world falls prey to the 'free market,' new enemies will continue to appear, and American society will grow increasingly fractured and divided against itself. For that is the way it has to be.

PART II

A Century of Illusions – The American Presidency, 1901-2001

For Fascism, the growth of empire, that is to say the expansion of the nation, is an essential manifestation of vitality, and its opposite a sign of decadence ... But empire demands discipline, the coordination of all forces and a deeply felt sense of duty and sacrifice: this fact explains many aspects of the practical working of the regime, the character of many forces in the State, and the necessarily severe measures which must be taken against those who would oppose this spontaneous and inevitable movement ... for never before has the nation stood more in need of authority, of direction and order.

Benito Mussolini, 1932

Chapter 10

The Boy-King, 1901-1909

Theodore Roosevelt, Jr. was born on October 27, 1858, from the union of two extremely wealthy and politically prominent families. His mother was Martha Bulloch (you may have heard of their stores) and his father was Theodore Roosevelt, Sr., a descendant of Claes Martenssen van Rosenvelt, who had come to America from Holland in 1649. Teddy, Sr. served as an 'advisor' to Union troops on missions to the front lines during the Civil War.

Young Teddy went missing for awhile beginning in 1872, a fairly common occurrence with future presidents in their early years and nothing to be concerned about. He is said to have stayed with a family in—of all places—Germany. Teddy was back in time though to attend Harvard University, from where he graduated in 1880.

Just one year after graduation, Teddy won his first election—to the New York state assembly—and was immediately made the Republican minority leader. He was twenty-three years old. By 1884, however, Teddy had had enough of politics and declined to run for a second term, opting instead to spend some time as a cowboy and rancher.

Five years later, President Benjamin Harrison plucked young Theo off the ranch (or wherever he really was) and appointed him the US Civil Service Commissioner. In 1895, he became the president of the New York City police board, where he waged a very public—but largely illusory—war on police corruption.

In 1897, at the ripe old age of thirty-eight, Teddy became the Assistant Secretary of the Navy under President William McKinley. This raises the obvious question of what exactly a cowboy knows about running the US Navy. Apparently quite a bit, as it turns out, and Teddy wouldn't wait long to prove the prowess of American naval power.

On February 25, 1898—performing in the capacity of Acting Secretary of the Navy while the boss was out of town—Teddy cabled Commodore George Dewey and instructed him to sail for Hong Kong to prepare to take actions against Spain. McKinley shortly thereafter asked Congress to appropriate $50 million for the US military to prepare for war.

On April 30, Dewey began offensive operations by attacking the Spanish Fleet in Manila Bay, thus beginning the so-called Spanish-American War, though this is largely a misnomer given that Americans actually did very little fighting against the Spanish.

The war had its origins in a Cuban uprising against Spanish rule that began in February of 1895, provoked largely by Cubans who had been living in America. By late 1897, the Cuban insurgents were close to defeating the Spanish, overthrowing some four hundred years of colonial rule. In December of that year, the battleship *Maine* was sent to the port of Havana, allegedly to protect US interests.

By that time, the newspapers of William Randolph Hearst and Joseph Pulitzer were shamelessly propagandizing for America to enter the war, allegedly to end Spanish barbarism and liberate her colonies. By January 24, the *Maine* had dropped anchor at

Havana; three weeks later, it exploded, killing at least 260 American servicemen. The sinking of the ship was immediately blamed on Spanish saboteurs, though decades later it would be acknowledged that the explosion was internal in origin.

At McKinley's request, Congress drafted a resolution calling for Spain's withdrawal from Cuba, which the president approved on April 20. Two days later, McKinley ordered a naval blockade of Cuba, prompting a declaration of war from Spain. The US Congress followed suit the next day, declaring war on Spain.

The much lauded Spanish Fleet was quickly dispatched by Dewey's naval assault. Within twenty-four hours, the fleet was in tatters and control of Manila Bay had transferred to the Americans, with no loss of life and only seven men wounded. By August, the Spanish had been driven completely out of the Philippines.

In May, Roosevelt resigned his post and organized a 'civilian' army known in American mythology as the Rough Riders, allegedly made up of other 'cowboys,' though the group was in fact largely composed of Ivy League aristocrats, the forerunners of the pre-OSS 'Old Boys' network. Teddy served with the rank of Lieutenant Colonel.

On June 14, Teddy's 'civilian' troops departed for Cuba from a staging area in Tampa, Florida, along with thousands of non-civilian troops. Many of these were regiments of African-American and other dark-skinned ethnic peoples, dubbed 'Immunes' because it was said that they were more resistant to yellow fever and malaria, which were likely to be encountered.

A more accurate name for these divisions would have been 'expendables.' They were used by Teddy as cannon-fodder to lead the charge—including the fabled ascent of San Juan Hill—with explicit warnings having been given the men that cowards and deserters would be summarily executed.

The fighting was over in less than a month, the formal surrender of Santiago coming on July 17. The Stars and Stripes ceremoniously replaced the Spanish flag which had flown for centuries; the Cuban flag, as well as representatives of the insurgency, were nowhere to be seen.

Prior to this time, Roosevelt had been known by the more formal 'Theodore,' but now he began to be regularly referred to as 'Teddy' in newspaper articles and cartoons, his exploits shamelessly romanticized by Hearst and others.

One of these was famed author Stephen Crane, who accompanied the Rough Riders as a 'journalist' to document their adventures. Thomas Edison sent camera crews to film the war, though the teams only filmed the troops preparing for battle. The actual battles were shot as 'reenactments' back home in New Jersey.

When Teddy returned to the states as the conquering hero, he quickly became the governor of New York. That didn't last long though, as the very next year he became the vice presidential running-mate of President McKinley, who was facing a re-election campaign.

McKinley had opted to replace his first vice president, Garret Hobart, a move that has been known to shorten the life expectancy of sitting presidents. McKinley was re-elected, and in March of 1901 Teddy became the new vice president. That was to be a temporary position, however.

On September 6, McKinley was shot in Buffalo, New York, allegedly by an anarchist named Leon Czolgosz. One bullet grazed the president's ribs and another struck his abdomen, though neither proved to be fatal. Nevertheless, McKinley died eight days later, allegedly of gangrene, and the boy-king became the 26th President of the United States. Within two months, Czolgosz was permanently silenced, having been tried, convicted, sentenced and executed.

Roosevelt's administration actively encouraged and incited a revolt on November 3, 1903, in the state of Panama, at the time a part of the nation of Columbia. American naval power prevented a suppression of the revolt, and just three days later, on November 6, the United States formally recognized the new nation of Panama. Work was immediately begun on constructing the Panama Canal.

In 1904, vying for a second term, Roosevelt was opposed for the Republican nomination by Mark Hanna of Ohio, who had been McKinley's principal backer and financier during his gubernatorial and presidential campaigns. This could have posed a problem for Teddy, but luckily Hanna died before the Republican National Convention and Roosevelt clinched the nomination.

During his second term, Teddy ordered the 'Great White Fleet' on a world tour as a show of US naval superiority – and American belligerence. Around this same time, he sent John Watson Foster, who had served as Secretary of State under President Harrison, to the Hague Conference to represent a Chinese government badly fractured by the Boxer Rebellion and the Russo-Japanese War. Foster brought along his young grandson, John Foster Dulles, who served as the delegation's recording secretary.

John Watson Foster had previously distinguished himself by encouraging an uprising against Queen Liliuokalani in Hawaii in 1893. American businessmen—with an assist from US troops—overthrew the Queen, setting the stage for the annexation of the islands. More US troops were deployed to support the illegitimate provisional government of Sanford B. Dole.

Chapter 11

Teddy's Alter Ego, 1909-1913

William Howard Taft was born September 15, 1857 to a prominent New England family of British ancestry. His father served as a judge, as the US Attorney General, and as Secretary of War under President Ulysses S. Grant. In 1878, young William graduated from Yale University and two years later received a law degree from Cincinnati Law School.

Just a few months later, Taft was appointed assistant prosecutor of Hamilton County, Ohio. By 1882, he was made Cincinnati's collector of internal revenue, and by 1885, the assistant county solicitor. Two years later, Taft was chosen to complete an unfinished term on the Ohio Supreme Court. He was not yet thirty years old.

After completing that term, Taft was elected to a full term on the bench, which he followed up the next year with an appointment by President Harrison to serve as the US Solicitor General. He was still just thirty-two years old. The next year he returned to

Cincinnati as a circuit court judge, where he spent the majority of the next decade issuing injunctions against labor leaders and unions.

In 1900, President McKinley appointed Taft to head a commission to bring 'peace' to the Philippines, where rebels led by Emilio Aguinaldo continued to actively resist American occupation. By the time they finished resisting, roughly a million of them would be dead.

In August of 1898, just a few months after the defeat of the Spanish Fleet, Spain had agreed to stage a mock battle in Manila and to thereupon surrender to the US, turning over possession of the Philippines. This theoretically should have ended the Spanish-American War.

The US, however, had no intention of leaving the 'liberated' country to its own devices. In October, peace negotiations began in Paris, with representatives from Cuba and the Philippines notably absent. A treaty was signed on December 10, with Spain renouncing her claim to Cuba, Guam, Puerto Rico and the Philippines, and ceding their ownership to the United States.

On February 6, 1899, the Senate ratified the treaty by the narrowest of margins, granting the US its first colonies. To ensure passage, which had appeared unlikely despite the enthusiastic support of such prominent figures as Senator Henry Cabot Lodge, American forces had provoked an attack by Philippine guerillas two days prior to the Senate vote. Fighting immediately escalated and continued for another three years.

This was not, as a brief aside, the beginnings of US imperialism, as is so frequently stated. Just seven years prior to this illegal extension of American sovereignty, hundreds of Lakota Indians—more than two-thirds of them women and children—were slaughtered by the US Seventh Cavalry at Wounded Knee in South

Dakota in the last of what were euphemistically dubbed the 'Indian Wars.'

Survivors were tracked down and killed one-by-one, though a one-year-old infant was spared and taken as a 'war curio' by General William Colby, to be put on display for profit. This act of genocide, and countless others that preceded it, would later provide the model for Hitler's *Lebensraum* policy, justifying the taking by force of 'living room' for the Aryan race. But here I digress.

In 1901, Taft was named the provisional governor of the devastated Philippines, with the full support of Teddy in Washington, who would become president before the end of the year. On September 24, just eight days after Roosevelt took office, Philippine guerillas armed with machetes attacked an encampment of US troops, killing forty-eight.

The attack was termed an atrocity by the new administration, and the American response was swift and brutal. Orders were given to kill anyone of gun-bearing age, and to turn the islands into a 'howling wilderness.' The death toll was staggeringly high. By April of 1902, the insurgents had little choice but to surrender.

Having 'pacified' the Philippines, Taft returned to Washington in 1903 to serve as Roosevelt's Secretary of War and 'personal ambassador.' Teddy stepped down after his second term and worked to ensure that Taft would get the Republican nomination in 1908. Franklin Roosevelt, though nominally a Democrat, aided in the effort as well.

Taft went on to win the election and in 1909 became the 27th President of the United States. He was to be only a single-term president however, as there was a war on the horizon and it's always best to have a Democrat in the White House under such conditions. To assist in that cause, Teddy entered the 1912 election as a 'Bull Moose' candidate, preposterously posing as a bitter rival of Taft.

With the Republican party split, Woodrow Wilson cruised to an easy victory. By 1916, Roosevelt and Taft were good buddies again. In 1918, nominal Democrat Woodrow Wilson appointed Taft—well known to be strongly anti-labor—to serve as the co-chairman of the National War Labor Board, convened to mediate labor disputes during World War I. Following that, Taft was next appointed the Chief Justice of the Supreme Court by President Harding.

Chapter 12

The Scholar Spook, 1913-1921

Thomas Woodrow Wilson was born on December 28, 1856 in Staunton, Virginia. In 1882 he obtained a law degree from the University of Virginia after having previously attended the College of New Jersey. Wilson subsequently settled in Atlanta, Georgia to open a law practice.

This proved to be short-lived, however, as Woody abandoned his practice a year later and entered the graduate school of the Johns Hopkins University. In 1890 he became a professor at the College of New Jersey, which six years later would become Princeton University. In 1902 he became the president of Princeton and his inauguration drew such notables as President Theodore Roosevelt and ex-President Grover Cleveland.

One of Wilson's students was John Foster Dulles, who enrolled at Princeton at the age of sixteen. Wilson granted young Dulles a leave-of-absence in 1907 to attend the Hague Conference with his grandpa. Four years later, Dulles joined Wall Street's Sullivan & Cromwell. He concentrated primarily on Latin America. As such, his most important client was the Panamanian government, to whom Sullivan & Cromwell had served as an advisor since the puppet regime's illegitimate conception in 1903.

In 1912, Wilson was touted as a contender for the Democratic presidential nomination, though his prospects did not look good. So weak was his support that it took a rather amazing forty-six ballots for Wilson to ultimately get the nod. On October 20 he resigned his post at Princeton and was victorious in the November election, thanks in large part to Teddy's 'Bull Moose' posturing.

In 1913, Wilson was inaugurated as the 28th President of the United States. Leading Company A of the Central High Cadet Corps in his inaugural parade was Captain John Edgar Hoover, eighteen years old at the time. Though it is claimed that Hoover came from humble roots, he would soon graduate as valedictorian from the prestigious school, situated in the most affluent section of Washington.

Following his graduation, Hoover enrolled at the equally prestigious George Washington University law school, allegedly attending nights on a work-study program while working days as a law clerk at the Library of Congress. Strangely though, the teenager from the wrong side of the tracks was given authority to establish an extensive new filing system at the Library, and was made House Manager of the elitist Kappa Alpha Fraternity on the university campus.

'Colonel' Edward House, a wealthy and influential Texan, served as the new president's key advisor and wielded enormous power in the Wilson Administration. On board as Secretary of State, beginning in 1915, was Robert Lansing – an uncle of John Foster and Allen Dulles. Lansing was brought on just after the sinking of the Lusitania on May 17, 1915.

As Secretary of State, he rigged the inquiry into the incident, suppressing various facts, such as that the Lusitania had been registered as a vessel of war and fitted with guns, and that she was transporting weapons at the time of the sinking. Allen Dulles joined his uncle at State that same year.

Wilson's father had been a Confederate sympathizer during the Civil War and the administration broke precedent by allowing segregation in the nation's capital. In 1915, with the Ku Klux Klan showing a major resurgence, D.W. Griffith's three hour *Birth of a Nation* became the first movie shown in the White House. The overtly racist work—based on the novel *The Clansman* by Thomas Dixon, a friend of President Wilson—was arguably the world's first propaganda film.

On April 6 of 1917, President Wilson belatedly entered World War I, though by the time US troops saw action the war was close to wrapping up. John Foster Dulles joined the State Department that year, serving under his Uncle Bob. Brother Allen was sent to Bern, Switzerland as an intelligence agent with the US Foreign Service, a role he would reprise near the end of the next world war.

By the summer of 1917, J. Edgar Hoover had managed to finish law school and pass the state bar exam. Through family connections, he was given a draft exemption and promptly put to work by the Justice Department organizing information on 'enemies of the state.' As he had in the Library of Congress, Hoover busied himself setting up a massive filing system to catalogue suspected dissidents. He was twenty-two years old.

In the fall of the same year, Wilson and House assembled a coalition of 'academics' in New York dubbed 'The Inquiry.' The group was headed by House's brother-in-law, Sidney Mezes, and included alleged journalist William Bullitt. This activity, likely not coincidentally, came directly on the heels of the October Revolution in Russia..

In 1918, President Wilson threw his support behind the US Senate campaign of native fascist and anti-Semite Henry Ford, who would later write *The International Jew: The World's Foremost Problem*, for which he was singled out for praise in Hitler's *Mein Kampf*. Despite the president's support, Ford was narrowly defeated.

In the summer of that same year, John Foster Dulles became the secretary and treasurer of the Russian Bureau, Inc., an intelligence front formed to pump money into the USSR in an attempt to smother the revolution.

In June of 1919, 'terrorist' bombs exploded in twelve cities across America, with one reportedly detonating near Franklin Roosevelt. The American media, already actively engaged in whipping up an anti-Red hysteria, had a field day. In response to what was portrayed as an act of 'communist' aggression, J. Edgar Hoover was put in charge of a new division of the Justice Department's Bureau of Investigation, the General Intelligence Division.

By October, Hoover's department had collected over 150,000 names in a rapidly expanding database. The following January saw the largest mass arrests in US history as the fascistic Hoover engineered the rounding-up of at least 10,000 Americans. There were widespread reports of severe beatings and forced confessions.

June of 1919 was also when Wilson took his much-vaunted 14 Point Plan to the Versailles Peace Conference, accompanied by various members of the Dulles/Lansing clan. John Foster Dulles came along as legal counsel to the US delegation, and brother Allen tagged along as well. Along with Admiral William Colby Chester, Allen was a leading proponent of seeking a reconciliation with Turkey, which had just finished up with an ethnic cleansing of hundreds of thousands of Armenians.

Robert Lansing was at Versailles as well, as chairman of the War Crimes Commission. His decidedly unpopular stance on war crimes trials nearly derailed the conference. Wilson's delegation found itself at odds with the group in other areas as well, including reparations payments.

The UK delegation brought a demand for $90 billion in payments from Germany, while the French sought even more – $200 billion. The US delegation, which also included Eleanor Lansing and Eleanor Lansing Dulles, took the position that $25 to $30 billion would be more appropriate, though secretly Wilson's team considered even that amount too high. The US prevailed and the final resolution demanded only $25 to $30 billion, paid out over thirty years. The fledgling Soviet Union was not amused.

Allen Dulles, meanwhile, was busy drawing post-war borders that included the carving off of the Sudentenland and its German speaking population. This would, of course, later provide the pretext for Nazi Germany to fire the opening salvos of World War II.

Other notables present at Versailles included Herbert Hoover and Robert Taft, son of William Howard. The next year, Colonel House appointed William Bullitt as chief of the Division of Current Intelligence Summaries. Allen Dulles was posted to the US Delegation to Berlin.

He was joined there in the fall by brother John Foster. Both were on hand for the failed Kapp Putsch, an early attempt to install a fascist regime in Germany by force. The coup attempt was led by 3,000 former army officers and NCO's.

While in Berlin, John Foster forged an alliance with Hjalmar Schacht, soon to become Hitler's finance wizard. Upon his return from Germany, Dulles was made a junior partner at Sullivan & Cromwell. That same year, William "Wild Bill" Donovan, a friend of the Dulles brothers since childhood and a representative of the Rockefeller Foundation, was sent to Siberia as part of a 'fact-finding' mission.

Chapter 13

The Short Timer, 1921-1923

Warren Gamaliel Harding was born in Corsica, Ohio on November 2, 1865 – allegedly on a farm. It is claimed that Warren entered Ohio Central College in 1879, though he would have been not quite fourteen years old at the time. Three years later the family moved to Marion, Ohio, where the seventeen-year-old Harding is said to have tried his hand at selling insurance, studying law, teaching school and working as a reporter, printer, and pressman for the *Marion Democratic Mirror*.

In 1884 the still-teenaged Harding and a friend somehow managed to buy a floundering rival of the *Mirror*, the *Marion Star*. Seven years later, Harding—having bought out his partner—married a wealthy and well-connected widow known as "Duchess," and with her family fortune converted the weekly *Star* into an influential daily newspaper.

Harding entered politics in 1898 when he was elected to the Ohio state senate. Two years later he was re-elected to a second term, and in 1903 ascended to the office of lieutenant governor of Ohio. Following a failed run for the governor's office in 1910, Harding gained a seat in the US Senate in the 1914 elections.

In June of 1920, delegates at the Republican National Convention in Chicago became deadlocked over the three leading contenders for the presidential nomination. A select group of 'conservatives'—including Henry Cabot Lodge—meeting at night behind closed doors in the Blackstone Hotel, broke the deadlock by bypassing *all three* contenders in favor of the freshman senator as a 'compromise' candidate. That meeting would give the country the phrase 'smoke-filled room.'

Harding went on to win the election and in 1921 became the 29th President of the United States, with Calvin Coolidge as his vice president. His administration soon found itself rocked by a string of financial scandals and rampant corruption. In February of 1923, Harding's close friend and head of the Veteran's Bureau—Charles R. Forbes—was forced to resign and flee the country after having robbed the government of some $200 million.

Harding's Justice Department—led by Attorney General Harry Daugherty—was enmeshed in scandal as well, enduring repeated accusations that officials were accepting bribes to overlook Prohibition violators. Daugherty was also reportedly receiving payoffs from BASF. In 1920, John Foster Dulles had advised the company—a Sullivan & Cromwell client—to declare bankruptcy to escape the Alien Property Custodian.

Yet another financial swindle, dubbed the Teapot Dome Scandal, involved Harding's Secretary of the Navy. In the midst of all this, President Harding set out on a transcontinental tour on June 20, 1923. He made it only as far as Vancouver, where on July 29 he suddenly collapsed. He was rushed to San Francisco's Palace Hotel, where he seemed to recover.

He again collapsed on August 2, only this time he did not recover. White House physician General Sawyer, who along with Duchess Harding was at the president's side, listed the cause of death as an embolism, though how he divined this without ever performing an autopsy is anyone's guess.

Approximately one year later, while being visited by Harding's widow, General Sawyer was likewise struck dead. His death, according to the *New York Times*, "was almost identical with the manner of death of the late Warren G. Harding when General Sawyer was with the President in San Francisco." Nothing out of the ordinary about that.

The very month of Harding's death, the Treaty of Sevres— which had been negotiated following World War I—was replaced by the Treaty of Lausanne, thereby abandoning any claims to an Armenian republic and granting amnesty to all the *Ittihadists* (pronounced *Nazis*) who had been convicted of war crimes in earlier proceedings. Allen Dulles, of course, played a key role.

Also in 1923, international banker J.P. Morgan recommended John Foster Dulles to serve as special counsel to the Dawes Committee, established by US and British banks to circumvent the reparation payment requirements from Versailles. Dulles masterminded a scheme whereby American and foreign banks made loans to Germany which it then used to pay the European powers, who in turn paid their war loans to the US.

For relieving Germany of the burden of actually making reparations payments, Dulles was, of course, hailed as a genius. 1923 also marked yet another attempt at installing a fascist regime in Germany, this time by way of the so-called Beer Hall Putsch. For this failed coup, it was sister Eleanor Lansing Dulles who was on hand, along with a large party of 'friends.'

In March of the following year, scandal-wracked Attorney General Daugherty was dismissed by Harding's successor, Calvin Coolidge. Daugherty was twice brought to trial in 1927, with both trials ending in a hung jury. He also—assisted by *The Clansman* novelist Thomas Dixon—later wrote *The Inside Story of the Harding Tragedy*, proclaiming the innocence of both himself and the deceased president.

Many did not buy Daugherty's protestations of innocence, however. In fact, a good number of Americans believed that the Attorney General was just the tip of the iceberg, and that many in government and law enforcement were profiteering off the Prohibition laws. This does indeed appear to be the case.

Many outside of government were profiting handsomely off the temperance movement as well, none more so than three men who—legend has it—first met in New York City in 1918. One of them was a twenty-one-year-old native of Sicily named Salvatore Lucania. Another was sixteen-year-old Maier Suchowljansky from Grodna, Russia. The third was twelve-year-old Benjamin Siegelbaum, a native of Brooklyn.

These three men—better known as Charles "Lucky" Luciano, Meyer Lansky and "Bugsy" Siegel—were soon to permanently change the face of organized crime in America. The trio (or more accurately, a silent partner by the name of Arnold "The Brain" Rothstein – better known for 'fixing' the 1919 World Series game) had a dream: to consolidate mob operations all across the country.

To do so, all of the old-school mob bosses would have to be eliminated – the so-called 'Mustache Petes.' In order to put their plan into action though, the three needed money – and lots of it. Therein lay the problem, for the 'Petes' had all the traditional rackets firmly in hand. How then were the boys to finance their grandiose takeover scheme?

Luckily for the gang, in January of 1920 a whole new racket was borne virtually overnight as Prohibition went into effect. This fascinating piece of congressional legislation is generally said to have come about as a result of pressure from the temperance movement. In truth though, temperance societies were active in

America as early as 1808, and a national temperance organization had existed since 1826.

Calls for prohibition, in other words, were certainly not unique to the 1920's. For whatever reason though, the so-called Roaring 20's were to become the decade of Prohibition. And no one was quicker to capitalize on that than the Luciano/Lansky/Siegel gang, which would soon include Dutch Schultz, Joe Adonis, Carlo Gambino, Vito Genovese, Alphonse Capone and Albert Anastasia, among others.

The group set about buying up real estate, as well as a bottling company, a printing company, and fleets of trucks and boats – quickly building a massive illegal liquor manufacturing, bottling and distribution network. They also began buying off local politicians and police officials. Before the end of the decade, New York City alone would have 100,000 speakeasies and Capone would have another 20,000 in Chicago.

Beginning in 1922, Luciano participated in numerous gang wars as the liquor-financed drive to consolidate power began. In 1925, he became the chief lieutenant of 'Joe the Boss' Masseria—one of the two rival capos who ruled New York City—though his loyalties remained with the Lansky gang. In 1929, largely due to the machinations of Luciano and company, the Masseria gang went to war with the Salvatore Maranzano gang in what was dubbed the Castellamarese War.

On April 15, 1931, Luciano ordered the killing of Masseria in a Coney Island restaurant and quickly joined Maranzano's rival faction as a top lieutenant. Five months later, Luciano likewise ordered a hit on Maranzano. With the Mustache Petes out of the way (and Rothstein as well, who was killed a few years prior), the new generation of gangsters held a summit conference in November at New York's Hotel Franconia.

They now ruled New York City – but they were just getting started.

Chapter 14

The Yankee Doodle Dandy, 1923-1929

John Calvin Coolidge was born on the Fourth of July, 1872. He attended Black River Academy, and then Amherst College, graduating from the latter in 1895. He next went to Northampton, Massachusetts to study law, gaining admittance to the practice in 1897 and opening his own firm that he would keep until 1919.

Beginning in 1898, Coolidge also became active in local politics, first as a city councilman. From 1900 to 1911 he served as a city solicitor, as clerk of the courts, as a representative in Massachusetts' legislature and as mayor of Northampton.

In 1912, Coolidge was elected to the Massachusetts state senate, and just two years into his first term became the president of that body. By 1916, Coolidge had left the senate to serve as the state's lieutenant governor, and two years after that became the governor of the state of Massachusetts. Continuing his dizzying ascent, Cal was chosen as the running-mate for Warren Harding in 1920.

Coolidge assumed the vice presidency in 1921, another office that he would remain in for just two years before becoming—with the death of Harding on August 3, 1923—the 30th President of the United States. Coolidge did not prove to be a tremendously popular president though. He won the Republican nomination in 1924, but may well have lost the general election had not Wisconsin Senator Robert M. LaFollette entered the race as a 'Progressive' candidate, splitting the Democratic vote.

Coolidge's administration proved to be strongly pro-business and was particularly lax on enforcement of anti-trust legislation. The administration also exerted strong economic and military pressure on at least ten Latin American nations, including Nicaragua and Mexico.

On May 10 of 1924, J. Edgar Hoover was named the acting Director of the Justice Department's Bureau of Investigations. He was not yet thirty years old. Coolidge had brought Bill Donovan on board the criminal division of the Justice Department, and it was he who oversaw the transfer of power to Hoover.

The year before, Donovan had married the widow of alleged socialist John Reed, with whom Wild Bill had had close ties. In 1925, Coolidge brought Frank B. Kellogg—of the First Family of the American eugenics movement—on board as Secretary of State.

That same year, Allen Dulles served as a delegate to the Geneva Conference on Arms Traffic. The next year, he was a delegate to the Disarmament Conference. Older brother John Foster accompanied Allen on both of these outings.

During that same two year period, Sullivan & Cromwell lost a series of senior partners. The first died suddenly in 1925. The next died in a boat on the way to the home in Cold Springs Harbor that Foster had recently purchased, near to that of his friend and neighbor, Charles Lindbergh.

The next in the line of succession to head the prestigious firm quickly announced his retirement—a seemingly very wise decision—leaving John Foster Dulles as Sullivan & Cromwell's new senior partner. Allen joined the firm that same year.

In August of 1927, nearing the end of his first elected term, Coolidge released a tersely worded statement from a secluded vacation spot in the Black Hills of South Dakota that read simply: "I do not choose to run for president in 1928," thus clearing the way for the candidacy of Herbert Hoover.

During the final year of Silent Cal's administration, Secretary of State Kellogg, along with French foreign minister Aristide Briand, drafted the Kellogg-Briand Pact, which bound signatories to forgo war and resolve disputes by peaceful means. This would prevent the United States from coming to the aid of Spain, China, and much of Europe as fascist movements quickly began sweeping across the globe.

Chapter 15

The Man From Nowhere, 1929-1933

Herbert Clark Hoover was, without a doubt, the spookiest president of the twentieth century. I have no idea who this guy was or where he really came from. He apparently was born on August 10, 1874 in West Branch, Iowa, and by the age of eight reportedly had lost both of his parents. He went missing for the next nine years, allegedly raised in 'Newberg'—a secluded Quaker settlement in Oregon—where he was put to work and was informally educated.

In 1891, he was improbably honored with admittance into the first freshman class at Stanford University. He graduated four years later and quickly thereafter went to work for a 'civilian' engineering firm in San Francisco. In 1898, Hoover was sent to Australia on the pretext of introducing California mining techniques and quickly became a wealthy man.

The next year he was transferred to China, just in time to be on hand for the Boxer Rebellion the following year (a nationalist uprising against European and Japanese influence). In June of 1900, Hoover and his fellow 'engineers' are said to have built a

protective wall to guard against attack from the Boxers while
President McKinley sent in thousands of US troops.

Later that same year, Hoover was sent to England and given a
20% stake in Bewick, Moreing and Company, an allegedly civilian mining interest with assets in Egypt, Australia, New Zealand,
South Africa, Canada and Nevada. He spent the next decade-and-
a-half travelling the world as a prominent 'mining consultant.'

With the outbreak of World War I, Hoover was assigned the
task of organizing the return of Americans stranded in Europe and
of getting food, shelter and clothing to homeless and hungry
Europeans – or at least that's what he officially was doing. In that
capacity, strangely enough, he frequently operated behind the
lines of hostile armies and moved freely through naval blockades.

In 1917, President Wilson brought Hoover back from Europe
and appointed him the US Food Administrator, a position that
allowed him to serve as a propagandist selling the nation's war
aims to the American people. At the conclusion of the war, he was
sent back to Europe to serve as the chairman of the American
Relief Administration—ostensibly to assist in the restoration of
Europe—and promptly began working to have the blockade of
Germany relaxed.

In 1921, Hoover found himself on the sponsoring committee of
the Second International Congress of Eugenics, and that same
year was appointed Secretary of Commerce in the Harding
Administration, though he managed to emerge unscathed from
the wholesale corruption of the period.

With Harding dead and Coolidge having graciously bowed out
of the race, the field was wide open in 1928 and Hoover picked up
the Republican nomination on the first ballot, despite the fact that
he had never held any elective office. One of his most enthusiastic
backers was Edith Roosevelt, Teddy's widow. Hoover went on to

win the election and in 1929 became the 31st President of the United States.

During the first six months of his administration, stock prices reached a frenzied peak. Buying stock 'on margin'—an exceedingly risky venture—had become all the rage, with some 300 million shares being so purchased, mostly by people who could ill afford to take the risk. The market soon crashed, casting adrift millions of formerly middle-class Americans, who had falsely assumed that their piece of the pie was secure.

A massive economic depression ensued, both in America and elsewhere, with the resultant social upheaval and concentration of wealth adding substantial fuel to the fascist movements developing around the world, including in the United States.

By 1932, social conditions had deteriorated considerably and some 10,000 World War I veterans marched on Washington demanding early payment on certificates issued in 1924. The US Senate refused the veterans' pleas and President Hoover sent in troops led by General Douglas MacArthur to forcefully evict the men with tear gas and bayonets.

Hoover did not gain a second term in the White House and relinquished the presidency to FDR in 1933. He remained a formidable force in US politics for nearly another quarter-century, however. J. Edgar Hoover, re-appointed by the allegedly unrelated Herbert Hoover, remained an equally formidable force for another forty years.

Early in 1938, the former president traveled to Germany to meet with Adolf Hitler, shortly before the Fuhrer kicked off the war by annexing Austria, followed quickly by the Sudentenland. The next year, Hoover organized a relief fund to help Finland— whose air force planes proudly displayed the Nazi swastika— defend itself against the USSR. Apparently it never crossed his mind to organize a fund to help any of the countries facing invasion by Nazi Germany.

In 1941, the former president held a series of secretive, high-level meetings in London, England. The purpose appears to have been to reach a negotiated peace with Germany, just weeks before the Nazi regime launched the massive invasion into the Soviet Union.

Immediately after the war, Hoover made a number of trips abroad, no doubt for purely humanitarian purposes, or possibly to consult on some mining projects. Following one such trip in 1947, he submitted a report strongly urging that I.G. Farben and Krupp—two of the largest industrial cartels that had fueled Nazi Germany—be enabled to spearhead the rebuilding of Germany.

Also in 1947, good old Herbie was appointed by President Truman as chairman of the Commission on Organization of the Executive Branch of Government, better known as the Hoover Commission. The purpose of the commission, as with various other actions taken by the Truman Administration in the post-war years, was to institutionalize the national intelligence state.

This was done in a variety of ways, including through the creation of the National Security Council and the Central Intelligence Agency, and by a reorganization of America's military services that thereafter placed them under 'civilian' control. In 1953, President Eisenhower called upon Hoover to again assemble a commission to further restructure the federal government. This second Hoover Commission would issue a report the next year reading:

"It is now clear that we are facing an implacable enemy whose avowed objective is world domination....There are no rules in such a game. Hitherto accepted norms of human conduct do not apply....If the United States is to survive, long-standing American concepts of fair play must be reconsidered. We must develop effective espionage and counterespionage services and must learn to subvert, sabotage and destroy our enemies by more clever, more sophisticated, and more effective methods."

The commission wrapped up its work by 1955 and the aging war-horse—who had emerged from nowhere to ascend to the very heights of political power—officially retired. He would live another nine years, passing away not long after the assassination of President John Kennedy.

Chapter 16

The Return of the Boy-King, 1933-1945

Feel free to stop me at any time if you think you may have heard this story already. Franklin Delano Roosevelt was born January 30, 1882 in Hyde Park, New York. Throughout his early life, Frank would frequently go missing during the summer, usually to Europe.

Like his cousin Teddy, Franklin was partially educated in Kaiser Wilhelm's Germany. On at least one occasion during his youth, he was taken to the White House to meet his father's good friend, President Grover Cleveland.

In 1896, Roosevelt enrolled in the exclusive Groton School in Massachusetts. After graduation he was admitted to Harvard where the penultimate Democrat promptly joined a Republican club on campus. In 1903, Franklin graduated from Harvard but chose to remain there as editor of the student paper. During one of his summer breaks from the university, FDR vacationed aboard the Kaiser's private yacht.

On March 17, 1905 (and this is where things really start getting creepy), Franklin married his cousin, Anna Eleanor Roosevelt. Another cousin, President Theodore Roosevelt, gave away the bride. Nothing unusual about any of that, though it does kind of remind me of an episode of *The X-Files* I once saw.

In 1907, Franklin left Columbia University Law School after attending for three years, but without obtaining a degree, though he had passed the state bar. He is claimed to have then gone to work as a lowly law clerk in New York City. He also joined the Democratic Party that year, though this didn't stop him the next year from enthusiastically supporting the presidential aspirations of the reactionary William Taft.

In 1910, Roosevelt was elected to the New York state senate. Two years later, he was re-elected to the senate but was promptly appointed Assistant Secretary of the Navy for the incoming Wilson Administration and resigned his senate seat and moved to Washington. The boy-king was just thirty-one years old and had no naval experience, at least not on the record.

FDR remained at his post until 1920, becoming a close friend of all the nation's leading admirals. As his cousin had in the Spanish-American War, Roosevelt steered the US Navy through World War I. His superior was Josephus Daniels, a follower of William Jennings Bryan – a frequent Democratic presidential candidate and Wilson's first Secretary of State.

In 1918, Roosevelt went on a three month 'tour of duty' during which he visited the Western Front in France. In August of 1920 he resigned his post to campaign as the Democratic candidate for vice president. Following that, he left politics, publicly at least, to become the vice president of a large banking firm.

Roosevelt returned to the political scene in 1928 as a candidate for governor of New York. He won the election and began his first term the next year. In 1932, FDR emerged as the Democratic presidential candidate and won an easy victory over the decidedly unpopular Hoover, thereby becoming the 32nd President of the United States.

Meanwhile, Adolf Hitler was appointed chancellor of Germany by Paul von Hindenburg on January 30, 1933. On February 27, the Reichstag (Germany's Parliament) was devastated by fire, allegedly set by a Dutch communist, though evidence suggests Nazi complicity for the purpose of driving hesitant Germans into the fold. On March 23, an enabling bill was passed in the Reichstag, granting dictatorial powers to Hitler.

* * * * * * * * * * * * * * * * * *

We now interrupt the regularly scheduled programming for this special update on the Lansky gang: by 1932, Lansky had organized the casinos in Saratoga Springs in upstate New York and Luciano had established total control over New York's narcotics, gambling and prostitution rackets. They had also begun taking their show on the road, consolidating power from city to city, and had eliminated over seventy old-school capos.

To aid in this cause, the gang had created an entity known as Murder Incorporated, a nationwide network of contract killers. The group would be implicated in thousands of murders from coast to coast before its demise in the early 1940's, many of them intended to facilitate the Lansky gang's ruthless takeover plans.

At the 1932 Democratic National Convention that nominated FDR, Lansky met with Louisiana Governor Huey 'Kingfish' Long and arranged to pay him $3 to $4 million a year for the right to control the gambling operations in New Orleans. By 1933, Lansky had expanded to Hot Springs, Arkansas, Miami, Florida, and Kentucky.

With this massive criminal enterprise firmly in hand and growing rapidly, the gang was no longer reliant on the revenues from the illegal liquor trade. And so it came to pass that on December 5 of 1933, Congress repealed Prohibition with the passage of the 21st Amendment.

Just months later, Lansky, Luciano and Louis Lepke met at the Waldorf-Astoria to organize the national crime syndicate. Lansky would later proudly claim to have modeled the new enterprise on Rockefeller's Standard Oil Trust. By 1970, he would be worth a mind-boggling $300 million.

Not long after this meeting, Lansky began making regular trips to Cuba to forge an alliance with Fulgencio Batista y Zalvidar, who was already being groomed for the presidency. By 1936, Lansky had a monopoly on gambling in Havana, which would be overseen by Santos Trafficante, and Luciano was cooling his heels in Clinton State Prison, having received a 30-50 year sentence.

Strangely, Luciano was allowed to have unrecorded visits from family and friends, and on one notable occasion even received a personal visit from the judge who had sentenced him. I guess that's why they called him Lucky. Siegel, meanwhile, headed off to Hollywood.

During this period of the early 1930's, J. Edgar Hoover was refashioning his bureau into a 'crime fighting' entity, with a media-stoked fear of gangsters being used to justify vastly expanded police powers for the state. Hoover instituted the first modern crime lab and began fingerprinting all Americans. His officers were given full arrest powers and were authorized to use deadly force.

The gangsters though that Hoover went after were not those of the organized national syndicate. It would be another quarter-century before the FBI Director was forced to admit the existence of organized crime. Until then, he consistently maintained that gangsters were a local problem best dealt with by local police.

Hoover's men instead busied themselves pursuing 'criminals' who were, at least in part, creations of the media. These were men bearing such unlikely names as Pretty Boy Floyd, Machine Gun Kelly and Baby Face Nelson. These were also men, in many cases, who stood in the way of the Lansky gang's takeover plans.

Hoover's department was renamed the Federal Bureau of Investigation in 1935, and began a period of rapid growth that would continue throughout the Roosevelt years. Around that same time, Hollywood began glorifying the actions of the bureau's 'G-Men' and their arch-enemies. In 1936, President Roosevelt had a private meeting with Hoover and signed a secret order vastly expanding the FBI's authority to spy on American citizens.

We now return to the narrative in progress.

* * * * * * * * * * * * * * * * * * *

Though Roosevelt would ultimately be elected to serve an unprecedented four terms, his administration was almost pre-empted before it began. On February 15, 1933, a man named Giuseppe Zangara attempted to assassinate FDR but instead shot Chicago Mayor Anton Cermak, who later died from his wounds. Zangara was indicted, tried, convicted, sentenced and executed in less than five weeks.

The primary opposition to the Roosevelt Administration initially was, interestingly enough, from the political left. FDR soon began implementing his much vaunted New Deal legislation, continuing to do so through 1938. He also sent America's first 'ambassador' to the USSR since the 1917 revolution – William Bullitt, who had been a campaign speechwriter for Roosevelt and had briefly served as a special assistant to the Secretary of State.

Bullitt's naval attaché, Admiral Roscoe Hillenkoetter, would later serve as the first Director of the Central Intelligence Agency. Bullitt traveled frequently to visit Ambassador William Dodd at the US embassy in Berlin, where Hjalmar Schacht and John Foster Dulles were frequent guests as well. One of Bullitt's accomplishments as ambassador was to instigate the breaking off of the Franco-Soviet Pact, which would have prevented Hitler from invading France in 1940.

In October of 1933, John Foster Dulles pled Germany's case in *Foreign Affairs*, the mouthpiece of the Council on Foreign Relations, for whom brother Allen served as secretary. Throughout 1932 and 1933, Allen—by then a partner at Sullivan & Cromwell, which had offices in Hamburg and Berlin—worked with DuPont to secretly rearm Germany.

In 1934, Roosevelt established the Securities and Exchange Commission to regulate the sale of stocks and bonds, with Joseph P. Kennedy as its first chairman. Also established during the early Roosevelt years were the WPA and the CCC, ostensibly set up as public works projects to offer employment to some of the nation's millions of unemployed men. These programs, it should be noted, closely paralleled the public works projects instituted by Hitler at this same time.

Together, these organizations would build the industrial infrastructure of the country that enabled it to arise as a military superpower. Roads, streets, dams, bridges and public buildings were built at a fraction of the manpower cost that such development would have otherwise required. The CCC in particular exploited the country's desperate masses by putting men from city slums to work in military-style camps run by US Army officers at slave labor rates.

In 1935-6, Wild Bill Donovan was authorized by Mussolini to tour the Ethiopian battlefields as the Italian troops plowed in. Shortly after that, he was on the front lines in Spain – on Franco's side, naturally. Following that, he was off to Germany to study tank maneuvers. John Foster Dulles was, naturally, an attorney for the Franco government, as well as for its financial organ – the Bank of Spain.

William Bullitt, meanwhile, had been reassigned by FDR as the ambassador to France. In November of 1937, he met with *Luftwaffe* chief Hermann Goering. Over the next couple of years, Roscoe Hillenkoetter and Douglas MacArthur, Jr. joined Bullitt's staff in Paris.

In 1937, Roosevelt began a massive naval build-up, asking for a billion dollar appropriation and then almost immediately asking for more. These appropriations would soon build a 'two ocean' navy, which the country had previously lacked. Also that year, Franklin Roosevelt, Jr. married Ethel DuPont, whose family had purchased Remington Arms in 1933 and forged a partnership with I.G. Farben to manufacture explosives.

In 1914, Percy Rockefeller had taken control of Remington Arms, and had proceeded thereafter to supply vast numbers of weapons to Czarist Russia to suppress the Bolshevik revolution. After World War I, Percy joined W.A. Harriman & Co. as a director, alongside the Harriman brothers and Bert Walker. Percy was the son of William Rockefeller, a brother of John D. Rockefeller.

The DuPont family was reportedly the driving force behind the fascist coup plot exposed by Smedley Darlington Butler in 1934, just three years before the wedding of Roosevelt and DuPont. The plan allegedly called for the ouster of FDR, and the imposition of an overtly fascist regime.

Given the close ties between the families, the 'plot' could well have been a sham to strike fear into the hearts of Americans, and to give the false impression that a coup was *needed* to convert the country to fascist rule. The current incessant warnings from the right-wing crowd that a declaration of martial law is imminent serve much the same purpose. While preoccupied with averting such a declaration, the fact that America is already a police state is largely obscured.

As World War II continued to heat up, Averell Harriman—Prescott Bush's business partner and fellow Nazi financier at Brown Brothers/Harriman—was sent to serve as FDR's special envoy to Winston Churchill, and later married the ex-wife of Churchill's son Randolph. Harriman would also serve Roosevelt as Lend-Lease Administrator from 1941-1943, and as the ambassador to the Soviet Union from 1943-1946.

By May of 1940, Roosevelt was asking Congress for massive appropriations for armaments. In June, he asked W.S. Knudsen of General Motors to coordinate American defense production (a rather odd choice given that the corporate giant had such close ties to Nazi Germany that James Mooney, the executive in charge of European operations, had been personally awarded the Order of Merit of the Golden Eagle by Adolf Hitler).

By September of 1943, the US would produce 53,000 tanks, 123,000 planes, 15,000 artillery pieces, 9,500,000 small arms, 2,380 ships and 15,000 landing vessels. In September of 1940, the administration secured passage of the Selective Training and Service Act, the nation's first peacetime conscription measure, which quickly swelled the size of US armed forces. Conscription at first applied to men aged 21 to 36, though by December of 1942 this was expanded to include men from 18 to 44.

Not long after the Nazi invasion of the Soviet Union in 1941, FDR and Churchill met secretly at sea aboard the *Prince of Wales* to discuss matters unknown. By the end of the year the US had officially entered the war, following the bombing of Pearl Harbor. By February of the following year, Roosevelt had signed Executive Order 9066, authorizing the internment of more than 100,000 Japanese-Americans on the West Coast in concentration camps.

The next month, FDR signed another executive order, making sweeping changes in US military organization by consolidating power into the hands of a select group of generals. Also created at that time by executive order was the OSS, headed by Wild Bill Donovan. One of the earliest applicants was Charles Lindbergh.

David Bruce, of the Mellon family, was assigned to London as station chief. James Jesus Angleton was sent to Italy, where he and his father—Major Hugh Angleton—colluded with the Vatican on behalf of the fascist powers. Allen Dulles was once again sent to Bern, Switzerland, this time as chief of the OSS station and as FDR's personal representative.

In January of 1943, Churchill and FDR met at Casablanca to agree on an initial point of attack, deciding inexplicably on Sicily. The decision did not, needless to say, sit well with the Soviet leadership. John Foster Dulles spent his time in 1943 penning *The Six Pillars of Peace*, a manifesto proposing a one-world future.

Facing his third re-election battle in 1944, FDR failed to heed the lessons of American history and dropped vice president Henry Wallace in favor of Harry Truman. That same year, Nelson Rockefeller was named as the Assistant Secretary of State for Latin America.

Wall Street's Frank Wisner, another charter member of the 'Old Boys' network, spent the last half of 1944 in Romania, as the Red Army rolled across the border. Romania had contributed thirty army divisions to the 1941 invasion of the Soviet Union. Rockefeller's Standard Oil had vast holdings in the oil-rich country.

In the summer of 1944, Eleanor Dulles was appointed to the State Department's German Committee. On October 31, 1944, President Roosevelt summoned Wild Bill to ask him to develop a plan for organizing a post-war intelligence network. The next month, Donovan submitted a proposal for the creation of a 'central intelligence service,' which would become the blueprint for the Central Intelligence Agency.

In February of 1945, Roosevelt tended to one of his final acts as president – attending the Yalta conference to meet with Churchill and Stalin. Averell Harriman was in attendance as well. Before returning to the states, FDR stopped to entertain King Ibn Saud of Saudi Arabia – a kingdom borne of a coup promoted by Allen Dulles and British intelligence asset Jack Philby. Ibn Saud had been a fully complicit partner of Hitler's Germany.

March of 1945 found Allen Dulles meeting with General Karl Wolff in Bern. The meeting had been facilitated by Pope Pius XII, who had previously met with the general. Wolff was the commander-in-chief of SS forces, and the highest ranking Nazi in Italy. He and Dulles conspired to find a way for German troops to surrender on the Western Front. These actions were, of course, taken without the knowledge of alleged ally Josef Stalin.

Wolff was, without question, a war criminal of the highest order. His troops had been complicit in a number of massacres, including the slaughter of entire villages. Wolff had also observed terminal human experiments conducted at Dachau, and played a key role in transporting Poles to the Treblinka death camp.

On April 12 of 1945, not long after Roosevelt returned from Yalta and just a few weeks from the cessation of hostilities in Europe, Josef Stalin cabled FDR accusing the US and the UK of seeking a separate peace with Germany, in violation of numerous promises. Later that same day, Roosevelt complained of a headache, lost consciousness, and shortly thereafter died. Harry Truman, who had served just 82 days as vice president, took the wheel.

Incidentally, there was an uncanny degree of symmetry between the final days of the Roosevelt presidency and the final days of the Lincoln presidency eighty years prior. Like FDR, Lincoln had faced a re-election campaign near the close of one of the most significant wars in America's history – the Civil War. Also like Roosevelt, Lincoln had dropped his sitting vice president (Hannibal Hamlin) in favor of a new running-mate (Andrew Johnson).

On February 3, 1865, Lincoln had attended the Hampton Roads Conference, to discuss peace terms. Roosevelt attended the Yalta Conference on February 4, 1945 to do likewise. In the waning hours of the war, Lincoln had been killed on April 14, 1865. Though the belief that John Wilkes Booth acted as a 'lone nut' assassin is actively encouraged today, the truth is that Booth was just the front-man for a much wider conspiracy, as was openly acknowledged at the time. Four additional conspirators were sent to the gallows.

Eighty years later, almost to the day, Roosevelt died as well, although allegedly of natural causes. The war in Europe ended just weeks later, with V-E Day declared on May 8, 1945. The President of the Confederacy, Jefferson Davis, was captured on May 10, 1865, signaling the effective end of the American Civil War. To Andrew Johnson, who had served just a few weeks as vice president and a few more as president, fell the responsibility of securing the final terms of the peace deal. Truman assumed the same honor, with approximately the same qualifications, eighty years later.

Chapter 17

The Return of the Man From Nowhere, 1945-1953

Harry Truman was born May 8, 1884 in Lamar, Missouri and promptly went missing, failing to attend school until the age of eight. Nevertheless, he managed to graduate high school by the age of seventeen and began the proverbial series of odd jobs, including allegedly working as a timekeeper for the Santa Fe Railroad, a mail clerk, a clerk for a banking firm, and a bookkeeper.

In 1906, Truman returned home to run the farm of his wife's widowed mother in Grand View, Missouri, where he remained for the next decade, 'farming' and investing in oil and lead. With America's entry into World War I in 1917, Harry enlisted in the US Army and was promptly named First Lieutenant with the Missouri Second Field Artillery.

Truman sailed for France on March 30, 1918 as a Captain in command of Battery D, an elite unit known affectionately as the Dizzy D. Not too bad for a semi-educated farmer barely out of boot camp. Truman returned in April of 1919, having achieved the rank of Major in less than two years of military service.

Back home, Harry opened a men's clothing store that catered to war veterans, especially members of his former unit. Three years later, Truman began his political career, thanks largely to the support of the notoriously corrupt Pendergast political machine. Also aiding the cause was the fact that Harry had applied for membership to the local Ku Klux Klan chapter.

His first elected office was as a county judge, to which he was sworn-in in January of 1923. By 1926 he had moved up to presiding judge, still in the back pocket of the Pendergasts. In 1930 he was re-elected to a second term, and four years later—backed heavily by the Pendergasts—he was elected to the US Senate.

Following his swearing-in as a freshman senator, Truman was quickly assigned to two key committees – the Appropriations Committee and the Interstate Commerce Committee. Nothing unusual about that. In 1940, campaigning for re-election with allegedly no money of his own and no outside financial backing, Harry nonetheless retained his Senate seat.

Immediately upon beginning his second term he was appointed to head a special investigating committee to look into the US defense program. For the next two years, the Truman Committee produced highly detailed reports on US defense preparedness as America readied itself to enter World War II.

In 1942, Truman headed a Senate committee looking into charges that William S. Farish—the president of Standard Oil—had actively been trading with Nazi Germany. Farish had previously entered a plea of 'no contest' to the charges, which had initially been pursued by the Department of Justice.

On March 26, Thurman Arnold from the Justice Department appeared before Truman's committee and presented a wealth of incriminating evidence against Farish and Standard Oil, including documentation that Standard had deceived the U.S Navy to pre-

vent them from acquiring vitally needed patents that had already
been supplied to the Nazi war machine.

Farish appeared on March 31 to rebut the charges, though the
evidence against him was overwhelming. By April 5 the hearings
were adjourned without having issued any indictments. Farish
retained his position with Standard as well as his spot on FDR's
War Petroleum Board. Before the end of the year though, he
would be dead. Six months later, his son—William S. Farish II—
was dead as well.

* * * * * * * * * * * * * * * * * * * *

We once again interrupt this narrative for yet another update
on the Lansky gang: beginning in 1942, the still-imprisoned
Luciano began receiving regular visits from agents of the Office of
Naval Intelligence, with Lansky acting as a go-between. They
sought to use his Sicilian connections to pave the way for the
Allied invasion of the island. Thanks to Don Calogero Vizzini—
the undisputed capo of Sicily—the invading troops met with
remarkably light resistance and quickly traversed the island. The
US Army rewarded Vizzini by appointing him mayor of Villalba.

On May 8, 1945—the day that President Truman declared as
'Victory in Europe' day—Moses Polakoff, Lucky's lawyer and a
veteran of Naval Intelligence, filed a petition seeking clemency for
Luciano. On January 3 of the following year, New York Governor
Thomas Dewey—after privately consulting with both Allen and
John Foster Dulles—granted Luciano's commutation.

Lucky was promptly deported to Italy aboard the *Laura Keane*.
Over the next five years more than 500 Italian-born gangsters
would follow him back—deported by the US government—providing the workforce for him to establish an international drug

empire which would dominate the global heroin trade for nearly twenty years and be dubbed 'The French Connection.'

Opium was harvested in Turkey, processed into morphine base in Lebanon, converted into heroin in laboratories in Sicily and Marseilles, and then shipped to the US by way of Cuba, the hub of the distribution network. The entire operation was overseen by Lansky with the Florida and Cuba operations run by the Trafficante family.

'Heroin' was, by the way, the brand name given to diacetylmorphine by Bayer Pharmaceutical Products when it got the bright idea to unleash it on the world in 1898 as a 'patent medicine.' An aggressive international advertising campaign was waged in a dozen languages touting heroin as a 'miracle drug.' Bayer was a subsidiary of the I.G. Farben chemical cartel, as well as the maker of those little orange aspirin your mom was always giving you when you were a kid.

In February of 1947, Luciano appeared in Havana to preside over a high-level summit of crime chiefs meeting to work out the details of the distribution network. In attendance at the meeting was Frank Sinatra, who also recorded anti-communist propaganda broadcasts for the CIA-front *Voice of America* that same year.

In 1949, Lansky embarked on a European tour aimed at forging alliances that would further expand the global drug cartel. His tour included a stop in Zurich to establish a network of numbered Swiss accounts to launder the drug profits, a system mirroring the one used just a few years before by Nazi Germany.

* * * * * * * * * * * * * * * * * * * *

In 1944, Truman was selected to replace Henry Wallace as FDR's vice president, and was sworn-in to his new office on January 20, 1945. Less than three months later, he took office as the 33rd President of the United States following the untimely death of Roosevelt.

The new president quickly re-appointed J. Edgar Hoover as FBI Director and sent Herbert Hoover on several trips abroad. He also sent Charles Lindbergh to Germany on behalf of the US Navy to inspect aviation facilities, including the infamous Nordhausen underground V-2 assembly lines where thousands of forced labor-ers had perished.

Fellow fascist sympathizer Averell Harriman was named as the administration's ambassador to Great Britain. He was next appointed by Truman to serve as the Secretary of Commerce, then as the 'ambassador at large' to Europe, and finally as the Director of the Mutual Security Agency.

On April 25 of 1945, the first United Nations conference opened in San Francisco with John Foster Dulles, who had helped prepare the organization's charter, serving as a senior advisor (the organization later gained a permanent home in New York, thanks largely to John D. Rockefeller, Jr., who donated the necessary land).

Also in April of 1945, Eleanor Dulles was sent to Austria to oversee post-war 'reconstruction.' She stayed in a 48 room palace and threw frequent lavish parties amid the bombed-out squalor of Vienna. Eleanor remained there until 1948, insuring that Austria was an early recipient of Marshall Plan funds. Some of that money was used to build new ski lifts and to refurbish winter sports resorts.

In early May, President Truman—in a classic case of sending the foxes to guard the chicken coop—assigned the OSS, still led by Donovan, to serve as the American component of the investigative arm of the International Military Tribunal in Nuremberg. Wild Bill himself served as an assistant prosecutor; one of his accomplishments appears to have been helping to assure the acquittal of Otto Skorzeny.

Allen Dulles headed to Berlin to head the OSS German station. Frank Wisner was second-in-command. Richard Helms, in the guise of a *United Press* correspondent, was on staff as well. Walter Beedle Smith served as the chief of staff at Supreme HQ; he would later serve as the CIA's second director. He also, along with Allen Dulles and Bill Donovan, approved the recruitment of Reinhard Gehlen's intelligence network.

In September, Gehlen was flown to the US aboard Smith's private plane. At the same time, Truman disbanded the OSS by executive order and replaced it with the Central Intelligence Group (CIG), headed by Lt. General Hoyt Vandenberg – a childhood friend of Allen and John Foster Dulles.

In October of 1945, General Patton was dismissed by General Eisenhower for openly calling for the resurrection of *SS* divisions to crush the Reds. This was clearly not the type of attitude that was approved for public consumption, though it was obviously widely held by US military and intelligence personnel. Patton was dead before the end of the year, killed in a car crash.

In late July, the Terminal Conference was held at Potsdam with Churchill, Stalin and Truman in attendance. The United States officially agreed to a tough policy of demilitarization, denazification and reparations payments, with the largest share to go to the devastated USSR. These pronouncements, however, were primarily for Western public consumption and to give false reassurance to the Soviets, as evidenced by the fact that by the next year Truman was steadfastly refusing to honor the reparations pledges.

Other early actions by the nominally Democratic Truman Administration included: admitting France into the 'Big 4' and allowing them to reclaim Indo-China, setting the stage for America's later involvement in Vietnam; issuing executive orders and court injunctions to end labor strikes; unifying the armed forces of America under a 'civilian' Secretary of Defense; and establishing the Atomic Energy Commission – thereby transferring control of nuclear power from the military to a 'civilian' entity.

On September 3, 1946, Truman approved the Dulles-drafted Paperclip Project presented by acting Secretary of State Dean Acheson, which would ultimately bring countless thousands of Nazi scientists, academics and doctors into the United States, including Dachau 'doctors' and chemical and germ warfare engineers.

The following year, the president proposed the Truman Doctrine, intended to send aid to anti-communist forces in Greece and Turkey and to manufacture a public consensus for fighting the Cold War. That same year, he announced the European Recovery Plan—also known as the Marshall Plan—allegedly intended to 'rebuild' Europe's markets. In the first fiscal year the plan was in operation, 28% of the funds went directly to Germany.

The initial sponsor list for the Committee for the Marshall Plan included Averell Harriman, Allen Dulles, Dean Acheson and Winthrop Aldrich. Aldrich was the son of powerful Rhode Island Senator Nelson Aldrich, who was the father of John D. Rockefeller, Jr.'s wife, Abby Aldrich, and the grandfather of their five sons: John D. Rockefeller III, Nelson Aldrich, Laurance Spellman, Winthrop and David

1947 was also the year that J. Edgar Hoover appeared before the House Un-American Activities Committee, lending a legitimacy to the group that had been previously lacking. The same year saw the passage of the Taft-Hartley Act, dealing a devastating blow to the forces of labor. The act was co-authored by Senator

Robert Taft, carrying on the anti-labor tradition of his father, William Howard Taft.

In the fall of 1948, a delegation that included Secretary of State Marshall, his deputy John Foster Dulles, Eleanor Roosevelt, and Dean Rusk, attended a UN conference in Paris. Dulles took command of the delegation and assured the recognition of the new state of Israel, with Nelson Rockefeller lobbying hard behind the scenes.

Dulles also attended the Moscow Conference in the post-war years, as well as heading the Carnegie Endowment for International Peace and serving as a trustee for the Rockefeller Foundation. In September of 1948, Frank Wisner was appointed to head the Office of Policy Coordination, a newly formed branch of the CIA created to conduct covert operations. That same year, against all expectations, Truman was granted a second term as president.

In the first year of his second term the North Atlantic Treaty was signed, creating NATO. Passage of the treaty was assured by, naturally enough, John Foster Dulles. In the summer of 1949, New York Senator Robert Wagner resigned, allegedly due to ill health. Governor Thomas Dewey, fresh from his presidential loss to Truman, appointed Dulles to fill the seat for six weeks.

Dulles was sworn-in on July 8; ratification of NATO hit the floor of the Senate just three days later. Dulles was the primary lobbyist for the treaty, and succeeded in getting it passed. He then made a run for a full term in the seat—the only attempt by a Dulles to gain elective office—and lost.

Shortly after, he was made a consultant to the Truman administration. In that capacity, he traveled to South Korea in June of 1950, to visit his old friend Synghman Rhee, the fascistic head of state. Dulles delivered a speech to the South Korean Parliament on June 19; just days later, South Korea provoked an attack by the

North Koreans. Without asking Congress to declare war, Truman promptly sent US troops under the command of General Douglas MacArthur to support what was euphemistically dubbed a 'police action.'

In August of 1950, Walter Beedle Smith, who was said to strongly resemble his Prussian grandfather, was appointed to head the CIA. He had spent the previous three years serving as the ambassador to the Soviet Union – a post he had inherited from Averell Harriman. Allen Dulles was appointed the Deputy Director of the agency, and Frank Wisner was named the Deputy Director of Plans.

On September 4 of 1951, Japan and forty-eight other nations signed a post-war treaty negotiated by John Foster Dulles at the behest of President Truman. That same year, younger brother Allen was appointed as the Deputy Director of the Central Intelligence Agency. Two months later, two Puerto Rican nationalists attempted to assassinate the president at Blair House, his temporary residence during White House renovations. The attempt failed but Truman voluntarily left office in 1953, having completed only one elective term and still eligible for another.

Chapter 18

The General's General, 1953-1961

David Dwight Eisenhower (his legal name, though he was known to all as Dwight David) was born a poor black child in Denison, Texas on October 14, 1890. Actually, Ike was quite white, though his parents were exceedingly poor – according to official biographies. Young Dwight was therefore unable to attend college after graduating from high school, so he went missing for a few years during which time he reportedly worked for his father at a creamery.

In an unlikely turn of events though, Ike won an appointment to West Point Military Academy in 1911 (in another unlikely turn of events decades later, Meyer Lansky's son Paul likewise received an appointment to West Point). It is claimed that he was not interested in the military and attended only because he could get a free education. Somewhere along the way though, he apparently developed a keen interest in pursuing a military career.

Eisenhower graduated from West Point in 1915 and by 1917 had achieved the rank of Captain and been assigned to train one of the US Army's first tank corps. The next year Ike was awarded the Distinguished Service Medal for his service during World War I, despite the fact that he had never actually shipped out.

In 1919, Eisenhower met General George S. Patton and began a long friendship. Three years later he shipped out to the Panama Canal Zone where he began a close friendship with General Fox Conner. Between 1926 and 1928, Eisenhower graduated from both the Army War College and the army's Command and General Staff School, both times at the top of his class.

By 1932, Ike had become the aide of General Douglas MacArthur, the army's chief of staff at the time. MacArthur stepped down from his post three years later to become the chief military advisor in the Philippines, a puppet state since the US invasion at the turn of the century. Ike accompanied the general as his chief of staff. By the time he returned in 1939, he was a Lieutenant Colonel.

On December 14, 1941, following the bombing of Pearl Harbor and the declaration of war on the Axis Powers by the US, Eisenhower was called to Washington and put in charge of the War Plans Division. By the following March, he was promoted to Major General and made head of the Operations Division.

In June, he was promoted to Lieutenant General and put in command of the US Army's European Theater of Operations. Two months later he was put in charge of Allied Forces for the North Africa campaign, dubbed 'Operation Torch.' On November 8, the first Eisenhower-led troops landed in Algeria and Morocco.

Just days later the fighting in Africa was called off, and French authorities in Morocco signed an armistice with the Americans. From then on, Ike spent a considerable amount of his time negotiating with the Nazi puppet regime in Algeria, led by Admiral Jean Darlan, which he agreed to leave in place in exchange for securing its alleged cooperation against Rommel's forces.

Eisenhower was harshly criticized for his actions but was nonetheless promoted to the rank of General. He was next chosen to lead the Allied invasion of Sicily in July of 1943 and the invasion of the Italian mainland in September. As previously noted, these operations required a close working relationship with the Italian Mafia infrastructure.

In December, Ike was selected to head the invasion of Normandy Beach, dubbed 'Operation Overlord,' and named the Supreme Commander of Allied Forces. Beginning in April of 1944, Eisenhower ordered Allied bombers to repeatedly attack targets in France—allegedly to prepare for the D-Day landing—though bomber commanders objected strenuously, preferring to bomb targets within Germany. Eisenhower prevailed though and a large swath of France was bombed, allegedly so as not to give away the landing sights.

On June 6, the D-Day invasion of Normandy by 156,000 men was launched. Right behind them were some 10,000 intelligence officers known as 'T-Forces.' In December, Ike was promoted to the Army's highest rank, General of the Army. On May 7, 1945, Eisenhower was in Reims, France for the formal signing of the surrender of Germany, ending World War II in the European theater.

Eisenhower remained in Europe for a brief time as commander of the American occupation forces in Western Germany before returning to serve as the army's chief of staff. He left that post in 1948 and, rather incongruously, served for two years as president of Columbia University. Following that, President Truman placed him in charge of the newly-formed NATO as Supreme Commander.

In 1952, Eisenhower—who, like Wilson and Hoover, had never held political office in his life—was tapped as a candidate for the Republican presidential nomination. With help from Richard

Nixon, he beat out Robert Taft for the nomination at the Chicago convention. Nixon, serving his freshman term as senator, was chosen as his running-mate.

With Harry Truman opting not to enter the race, Ike cruised to victory with a red-baiting campaign, becoming the 34th President of the United States in 1953. One of his first acts as president was the appointments of the Dulles brothers to head both the State Department and the CIA. Sister Eleanor was assigned to head the State Department's Berlin desk, and Walter Beedle Smith became Foster's Undersecretary of State.

Foster also brought Scott McLeod on board at State, resulting in a brutal, McCarthy-like purge of the department. Of course J. Edgar Hoover, who in 1950 had joined forces with Senator Joe McCarthy, was re-appointed to head the FBI. And William Colby, another OSS veteran, became the political operations chief in Italy.

Upon taking office, the Eisenhower Administration quickly dropped the doctrine of 'containment' of communism and adopted a more aggressive policy of 'liberation' of Eastern block nations. This was a policy more in line with that of one of Eisenhower's idols—Otto Skorzeny—whose picture Ike kept in his White House office. Ike also secretly warned the Chinese and the Koreans that he would "not be constrained" in his choice of weapons, raising the ugly specter of nuclear war.

In June of 1953, just five months into the administration and just three months after the death of Stalin, Kermit Roosevelt—chief of the CIA's Near East and Africa division, grandson of President Theodore Roosevelt and cousin of President Franklin Roosevelt—arrived in Tehran to direct a coup that he had planned with the approval of Secretary of State John Foster Dulles.

Brigadier General H. Norman Schwarzkopf—whose previous claim to fame had been leading the 'investigation' into the killing of the Lindbergh baby and the railroading of Bruno Hauptmann—was also enlisted by the CIA to assist in the coup campaign. From 1942 to 1948, Schwarzkopf had trained and reorganized the Iranian National Police. The resultant security force, SAVAK, would later be reported by Amnesty International to have the worst human rights record on the planet.

The Rockefeller family, whose Standard Oil had vested interests, helped out with the coup as well, as did the CIA's Herbert Hoover, Jr. – who put together a consortium to handle the marketing of all Iranian oil following the coup. The goal was to bring down Dr. Mohammed Mossadegh and install in his place Shah Mohammed Pahlavi, who not coincidentally had heavy deposits of his personal fortune tucked away in the Rockefeller-owned Chase Manhattan Bank, and whose father was an avid Nazi collaborator during the war.

The operation, code-named TP-AJAX, succeeded on August 19 and the CIA quickly pumped millions of dollars into the country to stabilize the regime. Shortly thereafter, Kermit Roosevelt was assigned by the administration to plan another coup, this time directed against the nation of Syria. Kermit was assisted in the operation by fellow CIA asset Archibald Roosevelt, yet another grandson of Theodore. Yet another member of the Roosevelt clan, FDR's youngest son John, had seconded Eisenhower's nomination at the Republican National Convention in 1952.

In 1954, John Foster Dulles and Richard Nixon urged Ike to intervene in Vietnam on behalf of the imperialist French forces and the president promptly invoked the 'Domino Theory' to explain the importance of Vietnam to the American people. An international conference was held in Geneva to establish an artificial division of the country at the 17th parallel; John Foster Dulles was present and accounted for.

The conference also promised free elections to the Vietnamese people in 1956, though these were repeatedly blocked by the US and never took place. Ngo Dinh Diem, who had been living in the US, was sent to serve as South Vietnam's Prime Minister, though the majority of the country's people were adamantly opposed to the artificially installed American puppet.

In June of 1954, the democratically elected government of Jacobo Arbenz Guzman in Guatemala was toppled on the decision of Eisenhower and the Dulles brothers. The Dulles-led CIA directed an exile invasion force supported by massive bombing and repeated nuclear threats. Arbenz had planned to nationalize the assets of United Fruit, which had close ties to both the Dulles brothers and the Rockefellers.

At the time, United owned the country's telephone and telegraph facilities as well as nearly every mile of its railroads, administered its only important Atlantic harbor, monopolized its banana exports, owned a huge portion of the land, and paid out over half of the country's total wages, while paying negligible taxes and export duties.

This deal came courtesy of John Foster Dulles, who had negotiated a ninety-nine-year lease for United Fruit in 1936. Financing had been provided by the Nazi-controlled J. Henry Schroder Banking Co., for whom Allen Dulles was both a legal advisor and a director. The Schroders were also full partners with the Rockefellers in a joint venture – Schroder, Rockefeller and Company, Investment Bankers. Senator Henry Cabot Lodge was a heavy investor in United Fruit as well, and was an active supporter of the coup.

Following the successful coup—which placed the country in the hands of fascist puppet General Castillo Armas—Beedle Smith resigned his post at State and promptly joined the board of United Fruit. In September of 1954, the Southeast Asian Treaty

Organization (SEATO) was created, another pet project of John Foster Dulles. The following year, Herbert Hoover, Jr. became Foster's Assistant Secretary of State, and Douglas MacArthur, Jr. became a top aide.

Also in the mid-1950's, Eisenhower began two new public works projects—the Saint Lawrence Seaway and the Interstate Highway System—further building America's military and industrial infrastructure. He also appointed the ever-popular Charles Lindbergh as a Brigadier General in the Air Force Reserve.

A raid on a home in upstate New York in 1957 resulted in the arrest of sixty-two crime bosses from around the country who had been convened for a summit conference. Following this discovery, J. Edgar Hoover could no longer deny the existence of an organized crime syndicate in America – though his bureau nevertheless continued to essentially ignore the problem.

On the first day of 1959, the US-controlled puppet Fulgencio Batista resigned and fled the country of Cuba in the face of a popular uprising led by Fidel Castro. Just weeks later, Eisenhower announced that: "I think we might as well understand this—might as well all of us understand this: I didn't say that nuclear war is a complete impossibility."

Ike, working with Allen Dulles, quickly began gathering exiles to build an anti-Castro infrastructure in Florida dubbed the JM/WAVE project. This exile community would be used by Santos Trafficante to replace Cuba as the hub of the Western heroin distribution network organized by Lucky Luciano, while Lansky's gambling operations were moved to Haiti.

To insure that Haiti remained firmly in American hands, US Marines and Naval ships were dispatched to the island by Eisenhower on August 12, 1959. They were accompanied by aircraft and helicopter support, all aimed at keeping the fascist regime of "Papa Doc" Duvalier propped up.

On August 18, 1960, Eisenhower approved a secret CIA guerilla war against Cuba, with Vice President Nixon playing a key role. That same month, Allen Dulles and Howard Hughes aide Robert Maheu enlisted Johnny Roselli—a Hollywood mobster and friend of Frank Sinatra—to help arrange a hit on Castro. To assist in the assignment, Roselli brought in Sam Giancana and Santos Trafficante.

Those machinations would result in more than two dozen assassination attempts being made on Castro's life by 1987, none of them successful. They would also result in the infamous Bay of Pigs fiasco early in the Kennedy presidency and decades of covert operations aimed at destabilizing Cuba. For Roselli, the result would be that his body would be found floating off the coast of Miami.

Eisenhower left office in 1961, having completed his two terms. In 1964 he lent his support to the ultra-reactionary campaign of Barry Goldwater. Four years later, he endorsed the candidacy of Richard Nixon, and his grandson David lent his own endorsement by marrying the president's daughter.

In 1970, David Eisenhower attended the funeral of CIA asset and torture aficionado Dan Mitrione, who had trained internal security forces in South America and been a friend since childhood of the infamous Jim Jones. Frank Sinatra—ever the humanitarian—staged a benefit show to raise money for Mitrione's widow.

Chapter 19

The Killing of the Boy-King, 1961-1963

John Fitzgerald Kennedy was born to a prominent political family in Brookline, Massachusetts on May 29, 1917. His father, Joseph P. Kennedy, had amassed a considerable fortune by the age of thirty, according to some reports due primarily to his ties to organized crime. At the age of thirteen, JFK was enrolled in the exclusive Canterbury School in Connecticut, but reportedly fell ill and went missing for awhile.

He reappeared at the Choate Preparatory School, also in Connecticut, from where he graduated. Following that, he enrolled at Princeton but again fell ill and again went missing. This time he reappeared the next year at Harvard. His father, meanwhile, was named the Chairman of the Federal Maritime Commission in 1937 by FDR. Joseph Kennedy was named the next year as America's ambassador to the UK. That summer, JFK and Joseph Kennedy, Jr. traveled to Paris for a week to stay as guests of Ambassador William Bullitt.

In September, Charles Lindbergh received a decoration from Adolf Hitler and the Nazi government and sent a well-publicized letter to Ambassador Joseph Kennedy praising the German Air

Force. In September of 1939, Frank Howard—a vice president of Standard Oil— flew to the Hague aboard a British Royal Air Force bomber to meet with Fritz Ringer of the I.G. Farben chemical cartel – a meeting approved by Ambassador Kennedy.

Upon Howard's arrival, Ringer handed over a bundle of German patents with the agreement that the two corporate giants would remain in business regardless of America's entry into the war and that Farben would get back its patents at war's end. Kennedy promptly arranged for the patents to be transported by diplomatic pouch to William Bullitt in Paris, and then on to William S. Farish in New York.

In 1940, John Kennedy graduated from Harvard and then briefly attended Stanford University's business school before dropping out and going missing down to South America, where Standard Oil facilities were supplying oil to lube the Nazi war machine. The following year, JFK joined the US Navy after a five month program of 'special exercise,' allegedly due to a back injury suffered in college that had originally kept him out of the service.

Two years later, Kennedy became the commander of PT Boat 109 in the South Pacific and—as the official biographies tell it—following the sinking of the ship by hostile forces, rescued a wounded crewmember by using his teeth to tow the man by his life jacket strap for three miles, then swam along a shipping route for four days before finally encountering friendly natives who carried his distress message carved into a coconut shell to a US infantry patrol. And with a bad back no less.

By 1944, JFK was back in the states working as a reporter for the Hearst International News Service. The Hearst papers were, at the time, deemed the "least fair and reliable"—and the most pro-fascist—of any in the country, according to a poll of leading journalists. In 1947, the war hero was elected to a seat in the US House of Representatives at the tender age of twenty-nine, where he would show an 'independent' streak by frequently voting with the Republicans in the House.

Five years later, he stepped up to the US Senate by defeating Henry Cabot Lodge in the 1952 elections. In the Senate, Kennedy notably failed to take a position against the rabidly anti-communist Joseph McCarthy. In 1957, JFK became a member of the Senate Foreign Relations Committee. He next served as chairman of the Senate Reorganization Committee, created to implement the reactionary proposals of the second Hoover Commission and translate them into law.

In 1959, Kennedy began his second term as senator but primarily focused on making a run for the presidency in the upcoming 1960 elections. Challenging Kennedy on the Democratic ticket was fellow Senator Lyndon Baines Johnson, with Kennedy getting the nod and choosing LBJ as his running-mate.

Aided by Frank Sinatra—working in collusion with Joseph Kennedy and mob boss Sam Giancana—Kennedy and Johnson prevailed over perennial losers Richard Nixon and Henry Cabot Lodge. Sinatra became a frequent visitor to the White House during Kennedy's tenure.

Later in the decade, Sinatra staged a benefit concert at Madison Square Gardens to raise money for New York crime boss Joseph Columbo's Mafia denial movement, which attempted to pass itself off as an Italian-American civil rights movement. He also switched parties and lent his fund-raising skills to Presidents Richard Nixon and Ronald Reagan.

Kennedy's first official act upon taking office on January 20, 1961 as the 35th President of the United States was to reappoint J. Edgar Hoover (a long-time friend of Joseph Kennedy) to head the FBI and Allen Dulles to head the CIA. Other cabinet appointments included Nazi collaborators Dean Rusk (the president of the Rockefeller Foundation) as Secretary of State and Robert S.

McNamara (the president of Ford Motor Company) as Secretary of Defense.

Named as an assistant Secretary of State and special 'roving ambassador' was Averell Harriman. Johnson, meanwhile, was assigned to serve on the National Security Council and visited some thirty-three countries in that capacity. With this new 'liberal' team on board, the administration quickly increased the number of 'advisors' in Vietnam from 700 to 15,000.

In April of 1961, just three months into the new administration, the disastrous Bay of Pigs exile invasion was launched and quickly crushed by Cuban forces, allegedly because the new president refused to authorize the use of CIA air support for the mission. The CIA's Chief of Operations at the time was OSS veteran Richard Helms.

By 1962, Kennedy was issuing warnings that US advisors in Vietnam would return fire if fired upon. On October 14, US spy planes spotted the first of what were reported to be ballistic missiles being assembled in Cuba targeting the shores of America. The United States had for quite some time had the Soviet Union virtually surrounded with ballistic missiles stationed in various 'friendly' countries.

Nevertheless, this tit-for-tat by the Soviets was portrayed as posing a grave and immediate threat to the United States, despite the fact that the Soviets appear to have been baited into deploying the missiles. In addition to the Bay of Pigs attack and the assassination efforts, JFK had staged a massive military exercise in April in North Carolina and Vieques, Puerto Rico, in which some 40,000 troops stormed the beaches. The high-profile provocations were clearly intended to signal to Moscow the intention to invade Cuba.

Kennedy announced the discovery of the missiles on October 22 while trading ominous threats with the Kremlin. For four days the country teetered perilously on the brink of World War III before the Soviets backed down, probably realizing that their American counterparts were just plain fucking crazy.

During this time of crisis, Kennedy was reportedly receiving 'vitamin' injections from his personal physician, Dr. Max Jacobson, that by some reports contained methamphetamine and/or cocaine. Dr. Jacobson would later become a regular at Millbrook, the estate owned by William Mellon Hitchcock that was used by Timothy Leary and company as the east coast headquarters of the LSD movement.

Mellon Hitchcock was the nephew of Andrew Mellon, who founded the Aluminum Corporation of America (ALCOA), Gulf Oil, and the Union Steel Company. Andrew Mellon was also appointed Secretary of the Treasury by President Harding, and served in that capacity through the next two administrations. In 1923, he introduced the Mellon Plan, resulting by 1926 in the lowering of the top income tax rate from 50% to 20% (can you say Reaganomics?).

Also in 1962, Allen Dulles was replaced as CIA Director, and Eleanor Dulles left her post at the State Department. Frank Wisner retired as well, and developed a habit of telling stories of the recruitment of high-level Nazis, including Martin Bormann. Wisner was shot in the right temple with a shotgun at the top of the stairs in his home. His death was ruled a suicide.

So was the death of James Forrestal a decade-and-a-half earlier. He had taken a dive out of a window of the Bethesda Naval Hospital in 1949. Forrestal had served as the Undersecretary, and then the Secretary of the Navy during World War II. William Bullitt served for a time as his special Assistant Secretary.

Forrestal had also served as a director of Brown Brothers/Harriman, as a vice president of General Aniline and Film, and as a vice president of Dillon, Read. Dillon, Read was yet another US banking interest that was directly complicit in financing the rise of Hitler. Like Brown Brothers/Harriman and Rockefeller's Chase Bank, Dillon, Read was a client of John Foster Dulles and Sullivan & Cromwell.

On November 1, 1963, the US-installed ruler of South Vietnam was assassinated, along with his brother, in a coup plotted primarily by Averell Harriman and Kennedy's Ambassador to South Vietnam and former foe, Henry Cabot Lodge. Three weeks later, Kennedy himself was assassinated in a Dallas motorcade, prematurely ending his presidency and traumatizing the nation.

Frank Sinatra quickly pulled from circulation his recently released film, *The Manchurian Candidate*, which depicted a hypnotically controlled political assassin. The film would remain out of circulation for nearly twenty years. On November 24, a man named Jack Ruby, who had ties to US intelligence and to organized crime figures such as Santos Trafficante and Meyer Lansky, shot and permanently silenced alleged assassin Lee Harvey Oswald before scores of law enforcement officers.

Two weeks later, Frank Sinatra, Jr. was reportedly kidnapped from Harrah's Casino at Lake Tahoe in what was the most transparently staged event imaginable. This quickly became something of a media circus and drew attention away from the unusual circumstances surrounding the killings of Kennedy and Oswald.

Four days after the kidnapping, Junior was released unharmed and virtually all the ransom money was returned. Normally press-shy Frank, Sr. threw a huge party, inviting all the press to attend – which they of course did. The case was tried within four weeks, keeping alive the saturation media coverage.

The kidnapper—a friend of the Sinatra family—was dealt a harsh sentence, yet served only four-and-half years and quickly reestablished himself in financial circles. He recently told a reporter that he and Frank, Jr. now occasionally cross paths, as they tend to travel in the same social circles.

While this fiasco was playing out, President Johnson created the Warren Committee in an attempt to lay to rest any doubts about the assassination of Kennedy. In September of 1964, the committee—which included such luminaries as Allen Dulles, Gerald R. Ford and John J. McCloy—released its findings, confirming official reports that Oswald had acted alone in the killing.

There is a certain irony in the fact that the panel contained both Dulles and McCloy. As High Commissioner of Germany in 1951, McCloy had signed an order freeing the majority of Nazi war criminals who had earlier been convicted at Nuremberg. They had served just a few years for committing some of the most heinous crimes of the twentieth century. It will be recalled that Dulles served much the same role after World War I. McCloy is notable as well for the fact that he had sat in Adolf Hitler's box at the Berlin Olympic games at the personal invitation of Rudolph Hess and Hermann Goering. He had also served for a year as an advisor to the Mussolini regime.

Chapter 20

The Enforcer, 1963-1969

Lyndon Baines Johnson was allegedly born into poverty on August 27, 1908, and in 1924 he graduated from Johnson City High School in Johnson City, Texas as one of six seniors – many of whom, it can be safely assumed, were named Johnson. Lyndon was only sixteen at the time and would have been, one would think, two years short of completing high school.

Following his premature graduation he went missing for a period of several years, during which time it is rather preposterously claimed that he 'drifted,' working at a variety of menial jobs – including picking fruit, washing cars, doing manual labor on a highway crew and helping out in a restaurant. His drifting days behind him, LBJ next enrolled in Southwest Texas Teachers College in 1927.

After just one year the former dishwasher left to take a job as principal at a school for Mexican children. Following a year of that, Johnson returned to Teachers College from where he graduated in 1930, despite the fact that he had attended for—at most—two years. He followed that up with a brief stint as a high school teacher.

Shortly thereafter, he left teaching altogether and signed on as the private secretary of prominent Texas Congressman Richard

M. Kleberg. From that position, Johnson would quickly ascend to the heights of political power – aided every step of the way by the conveniently timed misfortune of others. In 1937 he got his first big break when a House seat was left vacant by the sudden death of its former occupant.

LBJ ran in a special election to fill the seat and won. Prior to taking office, he was taken for a trip aboard the presidential train with FDR, and after swearing-in was immediately appointed to the Naval Affairs Committee and given ready access to the president. The former drifter was not yet thirty years old.

Four years later, another untimely death left one of Texas' Senate seats open. Johnson quickly announced his candidacy and received the full backing of President Roosevelt, who called the 33-year-old former fruit picker "a very old, old friend of mine." Apparently FDR spent some time in the orchards as well. Nevertheless, Johnson lost the election to Governor W. Lee O'Daniel.

Following this temporary setback, the congressman went into uniform with the US Naval Reserve and served for seven months with the rank of lieutenant commander. Having apparently become an expert on the US Navy, Johnson returned to Washington to head a special investigating subcommittee of the Naval Affairs Committee.

In 1948, career politician O'Daniel—having reached the exalted ranks of the US Senate—opted for no apparent reason not to seek re-election, despite holding a commanding lead in public opinion polls. The most likely explanation for this is, of course, that O'Daniel was threatened and/or compromised and thereby forced into stepping down. Such events, though, are never questioned in the telling of US history. At any rate, this act of generosity by O'Daniel allowed Johnson to make a second attempt at the Senate seat.

Even with O'Daniel out of the way, Johnson trailed opponent Coke Stevenson badly in the first primary. And when you can't out-poll a guy named Coke, your political career is in serious trouble. Much of Johnson's unpopularity was due to the fact that while he was supposed to be a Democrat, he had nevertheless voted the previous year for the ultra-reactionary Taft-Hartley Labor Act and had voiced strong opposition to civil rights legislation.

Miraculously though, Johnson managed to pull off an upset victory, stealing the election (quite likely literally) by just eighty-seven votes. An incensed Stevenson challenged the victory in court, but Johnson prevailed and was sworn in the next year as a US Senator and immediately appointed to the Armed Services Committee.

Just two years later, the freshman senator and former drifter from Johnson City became the Democratic whip when the Senate majority leader, entrenched incumbent Scott Lucas, unexpectedly lost his seat and the previous whip moved up to fill it. Two years after that, the new leader (now the minority leader)—entrenched incumbent Ernest McFarland—lost *his* seat unexpectedly. The former car washer who had yet to finish his first term in the Senate was now its minority leader.

In 1953, Johnson set about changing a longstanding Senate tradition by ensuring that all the newer 'Democratic' senators received at least one coveted committee assignment. In order to achieve this goal, LBJ is said to have 'persuaded' a number of senior senators to 'voluntarily' step down. Apparently he made them an offer they couldn't refuse.

By 1955, with LBJ just beginning his second term, the Democrats had taken control of the Senate making Johnson the majority leader, arguably the most powerful man on the hill. On July 2, he allegedly suffered a massive coronary in Virginia and was taken to Bethesda Naval Hospital, where he remained for several weeks. From there he went missing to his Texas ranch, where he stayed in seclusion for the rest of the year.

In 1960 he challenged John Kennedy in the Democratic presidential primary, losing out but signing on as JFK's running-mate. As vice president, Johnson served on the National Security Council and as chairman of the National Aeronautics and Space Council. He also enthusiastically backed US involvement in Vietnam, just as he had backed involvement in Korea as a senator.

Three years later, Johnson took his final step up the political ladder when another man died unexpectedly in office – President Kennedy. After serving the last year of Kennedy's term, LBJ gained re-election, largely as a result of the ultra-reactionary campaign waged by his opponent—Barry Goldwater—that proved to be very unpopular with voters.

In truth though, Johnson's views were not far from Goldwater's, as evidenced by his telling the Greek ambassador on one notable occasion: "fuck your Parliament and your Constitution. America is an elephant. Cyprus is a flea....If your Prime Minister gives me talk about Democracy, Parliament and Constitutions, he, his Parliament and his Constitution may not last very long."

Johnson also supported a coup attempt in Indonesia that left from 500,000 to 1,000,000 dead, and sent the US Marines into the Dominican Republic to put down a popular uprising against the puppet military regime earlier installed by the United States. And in February of 1965, regular bombing runs over North Vietnam began. By year's end, nearly 200,000 US troops had been dispatched to the region.

Though by this time it was little more than a formality, Johnson also was quick to re-appoint FBI Director J. Edgar Hoover, who was a close friend and longtime Washington neighbor. Following the disappearance of three civil rights workers in the mid-1960's, Hoover opened a new FBI office in the racially charged South.

Hoover's interest though was not in protecting the rights of the activists, but rather in infiltrating those movements and gathering intelligence. His men would likewise infiltrate the growing anti-war movement and the revolutionary Black Panther and American Indian Movements.

To ensure the continuation of these operations, LBJ waived the mandatory retirement provision for the aging FBI Director, effectively making him the head of the agency for life. Johnson also sent the allegedly retired Allen Dulles, along with his protégé William Buckley, down South to 'investigate' the violence being perpetrated against civil rights workers.

LBJ's political career ended in 1968 in a way that was in striking contrast to his prior actions. The consummate political animal—who had ascended to the top of the heap by apparently doing anything and everything necessary to get there—made the startling decision not to seek a second term of office, thereby clearing the way for the ascent of Richard Nixon.

Chapter 21

The Sacrificial Lamb, 1969-1974

Richard Milhouse Nixon was born to a family of Quakers in Yorba Linda, California on January 9, 1913. After attending Whittier College, a Quaker institution, he graduated from Duke University Law School in 1936. Dick then went to work for a prominent local law firm.

Around 1941, with America's entry into World War II, Nixon joined the US Navy and spent most of his time on a South Pacific island, leaving the service in 1946 as, naturally enough, a lieutenant commander. In 1945, he had been assigned to review captured Nazi documents, working closely with Allen Dulles to bury files that would reveal Dulles' clients to be Nazis.

Upon his return home, he campaigned for a seat in the US Congress, running a red-baiting campaign financed by Allen Dulles. Tricky Dick prevailed and in 1947 joined the House of Representatives where, as a 33-year-old freshman congressman, he served on the House Education and Labor Committee helping to draft the Taft-Hartley Act and on a special committee helping to establish the European Recovery Program.

That same year, the Dulles brothers took young Nixon on a tour of fascist 'freedom fighter' cells operating in post-war Germany. Nixon also developed a close relationship with his next-door neighbor, Walter Bedell Smith. Dick and Pat also became frequent dinner guests at the home of John Foster and Janet Dulles.

In 1948, Whittaker Chambers—a writer and editor for *Time* magazine—went before Nixon's House Un-American Activities Committee and accused State Department official Alger Hiss of being a communist. Following his re-election, with help from J. Edgar Hoover, Nixon spent the bulk of his second term relentlessly pursuing the Hiss case, gaining national exposure in the process. Foster Dulles consulted frequently with Nixon on the case, and even appeared as a witness.

In 1950, Nixon entered the race for the US Senate, again waging a viscous red-baiting campaign. This would be the last election victory for Nixon for eighteen years. He was sworn-in the next year as a freshman senator from California. That same year, Senator Nixon helped set up the Western Tube Company in Whittier, California in conjunction with a virulently fascist Romanian industrialist named Nicolae Malaxa.

Malaxa had entered the country with the assistance of Nixon, who then pushed for a private Senate bill that allowed Malaxa to remain in the US permanently. Their joint venture—which shared an address with the law firm of Bewley, Knoop, and Nixon—was an entirely fictitious entity. Nevertheless, Nixon secured for Malaxa a multi-million dollar tax write-off for a factory which didn't exist.

In 1952, the fledgling senator was chosen as the vice presidential running-mate of General Eisenhower. Between the two candidates, they had served a grand total of five years in elective office. Nixon was just thirty-nine years old. Not surprisingly, he again spearheaded a red-baiting campaign.

The campaign also actively recruited from among the pro-fascist groups that had been displaced by the war and given safe haven in America. During the first year of the new administration, immigration laws were changed to openly admit Nazi Party members and even former *SS* personnel.

Nixon repeated the red-baiting campaign performance in 1956 when the team came up for re-election. He spent a good portion of his eight year term as vice president travelling abroad, reputedly as a 'goodwill' ambassador.

In 1960, running on his own for the first time in a decade, Nixon lost the presidential race to the Kennedy/Johnson ticket. He followed this up in 1962 with a loss to Edmund G. Brown in the race for the governor's seat in California. Dickey was quickly garnering a reputation of being unelectable.

There was to be no stopping him in 1968, however. His main Democratic opponent, Robert F. Kennedy, went and got himself killed by yet another 'lone nut' assassin before he could even make it to the Democratic Convention. His alleged assassin, Sirhan Bishara Sirhan, had been a former 'patient' of CIA hypnotist William Jennings Bryan.

This left the Democratic Party with Hubert Humphrey as the standard-bearer, a considerably weaker candidate then Kennedy. To stack the deck just a bit further, nominal Democrat George Wallace entered the race as an Independent, splitting the Democratic vote.

As part of his campaign strategy, Nixon recruited the leaders of numerous pro-fascist émigré groups—most of whom had been recruited and brought to America as part of the CIA's post-World War II Paperclip Project—to form what was euphemistically dubbed an 'Ethnic Committee.'

After Nixon's electoral victory, this committee became the Heritage section of the Republican National Committee. In charge of organizing this operation was a man named George Bush. In 1969, Richard Nixon assumed office as the 37th President of the United States. One of his first appointments was Henry Kissinger as head of the National Security Council. Another was, of course, J. Edgar Hoover as FBI Director.

Kissinger had been born in 1923 in Furth, Germany, and had come to the US in 1938, allegedly to escape Nazi persecution. He had served during World War II in the 970th Counter Intelligence Corps, and served as well in the post-war military government of Germany, where he kept all the files on the recruitment of Nazis by US intelligence services. In 1954, Kissinger had received a Ph.D. from Harvard and joined the faculty, working on an intelligence program to recruit foreign students and serving as a high level consultant to CIA Director Allen Dulles.

In 1957, Henry introduced the notion of 'winnable nuclear war,' and in 1959 he became the director of the Defense Studies Program at Harvard, serving as a consultant to the Eisenhower, Kennedy and Johnson Administrations and conducting various studies for the Rockefeller Brother's Fund, established by the five sons of John D. Rockefeller, Jr. and Abby Aldrich. Kissinger was also reportedly an associate of Meyer Lansky.

Nixon took office amid promises to end the war in Vietnam, to which over 500,000 US troops were already committed. In June of 1969, he made a token gesture at doing so, withdrawing 25,000 troops. It was soon apparent, however, that the administration was planning to greatly escalate the war.

In April of 1970, Nixon authorized a massive invasion of Cambodia by US and ARVN ground forces – an operation engineered by Kissinger which set the stage for the rise on April 17, 1975 of the Khmer Rouge and Pol Pot. Before it was all over, well over a million Cambodians were dead.

In September of the same year, Nixon, Kissinger and CIA Director Richard Helms met to discuss how to 'save' Chile and decided to "make the economy scream" at any cost. The result was a bloody coup that ousted democratically elected President Salvador Allende and replaced his administration with a fascist regime led by General Augusto Pinochet.

Helms had been the CIA's director since 1966, appointed by Johnson and retained by Nixon. Thirty years before that, Helms—ostensibly a reporter for the *United Press*—had landed an exclusive interview with Adolf Hitler. In 1942, he was one of Donovan's earliest recruits to serve in the OSS. He was also a longtime friend of the Mellon family, and was a frequent guest at the Virginia estate of Paul Mellon.

In June of 1971, Nixon told Congress that he was declaring a 'war on drugs,' a war that would destroy countless American lives for the next thirty years. He also authorized an invasion into Laos that same year, expanding the war in Southeast Asia yet further. Hundreds of thousands more lives would be lost in Laos.

By 1971, public pressure was building for Hoover to finally step down from the FBI post he had held for forty-seven years, through eight presidential administrations. Early in the year, details of Hoover's *Gestapo* tactics and domestic intelligence operations had been publicized following a break-in at an FBI field office that yielded incriminating documents.

Hoover though was not quite ready to cede power, and Nixon allegedly shied away from replacing him. The problem was solved when the aging fascist was found dead just days short of his forty-eighth anniversary as director. The cause of death was listed as due to previously undiagnosed heart disease.

In 1972, Nixon cruised to re-election and shortly thereafter announced on nationwide television that peace had been reached in Vietnam. The agreement had been negotiated by Henry

Kissinger and David Bruce – a son-in-law of Paul Mellon who had worked for the Harriman empire in the 1920's. At least two million lives had been taken in Vietnam, in addition to the death toll in Laos and Cambodia.

In 1973, Nixon appointed William Colby as his new CIA Director. Colby had served in the OSS during World War II, and as the CIA station chief in Italy after the war, a hotbed of covert activity. In the late 1960's, he had run the notorious Phoenix Program in Vietnam, a torture and assassination program modeled after the Nazi *Einsatzgruppen* death squads.

Dark clouds were soon to form over the Nixon presidency as the specter of Watergate began to rear its ugly head. It began as a seemingly inconsequential break-in by a special unit known as the 'Plumbers'—created by Henry Kissinger following the leaking of the Pentagon Papers—and it ended with the downfall of the Nixon Administration, by all appearances as the result of exemplary investigative journalism and the smooth functioning of the government's built-in system of checks and balances.

A more thorough review of the debacle reveals a slightly different scenario, however. Much of the evidence indicates that Nixon was set-up from within, rather than caught and then pressured from the outside, not the least significant of which is the fact that the man who broke the story—Bob Woodward—was a briefer for the Office of Naval Intelligence shortly before becoming the cub reporter who got the scoop (his editor, Ben Bradlee, and his publisher, Katherine Graham, had close ties to the intelligence community as well).

After waging a determined battle to save his presidency, Nixon ultimately opted to step down on August 9 of 1974. He had announced his resignation the day before, upon the urging of Secretary of State Henry Kissinger. America was once again left with deep feelings of distrust and disillusionment. Gerald Ford, who had been appointed by Nixon to replace the embattled Spiro Agnew, succeeded the fallen president and on September 9 granted him an unconditional pardon.

Chapter 22

The Manchurian President, 1974-1977

Leslie Lynch King, Jr. was born on July 14, 1913 in Omaha, Nebraska. He graduated from the University of Michigan in 1935 and then inexplicably changed his name to Gerald Rudolph Ford, Jr.—although he allegedly bore no relation to Gerald Rudolph Ford, Sr.—before enrolling at Yale University to study law.

While attending Yale, the newly christened Ford signed on as a boxing coach, though he had reportedly never boxed in his life. Ford graduated from Yale in 1941, though why it took him six years to do so is anyone's guess. Following his graduation, Gerry opened a law firm with a friend from college.

This proved to be extremely short-lived, however, as by December of 1941 Ford had enlisted in the US Navy. He served aboard an aircraft carrier during the war, returning home afterwards as—you guessed it—a full lieutenant. He followed this up with a brief stint as a male model, during which time he roomed with Harry Conover – modeling entrepreneur and husband of famed cover girl Candy Jones.

Jones—with the help of her amateur hypnotist husband, a well known and highly regarded radio personality named Long John Nebel—would later discover that her own modeling career was a cover for her duties as a hypnotically controlled CIA agent. A book detailing Jones' experiences was published in 1976, shortly after which she was publicly linked to CIA hypnotist William Jennings Bryan. Bryan promptly turned up dead in a Las Vegas hotel room.

In 1948, King (oops, I meant to say Ford) was elected to the US Congress to represent Michigan and shortly afterwards married one of Conover's cover girls. He was immediately assigned to the subcommittee that appropriates funds for the CIA and also received assignments to several other influential subcommittees. He would remain there for the next twenty-five years.

In 1963, Ford was elected to chair the House Republican Caucus and later that year was selected to serve on the Warren Committee and appointed its official spokesman, lending his approval to the shamelessly transparent cover-up that passed for the official explanation of the assassination of John Kennedy.

Ford became the minority leader of the House in 1965, where he remained until he was selected by Richard Nixon to replace the integrity-challenged Spiro Agnew as vice president on October 11, 1973. Two months later, Ford was officially sworn-in to his new office.

On August 9, 1974, the disgraced Nixon stepped down and Ford or King or whatever his name is became the 38th President of the United States, the first man to assume the job who had been elected neither president nor vice president. To fill the office of vice president he chose Nelson Rockefeller, who had served as the OSS station chief in South America during the war, filling Nazi tankers with Standard Oil-produced aviation fuel and leasing office space to the local Nazi party.

Rockefeller's four brothers—John, David, Winthrop and Laurance—served in World War II as well, two in the Navy and two in the Army. All were undoubtedly intelligence assets. David later chaired the Council on Foreign Relations (CFR) beginning in 1970, and founded the offshoot Tri-Lateral Commission (TLC) in 1973 with Zbigniew Brzezinski.

Five months after taking office, Ford appointed a commission—chaired by Nelson Rockefeller and including California Governor Ronald Reagan—to investigate numerous allegations of CIA abuses. Not surprisingly, the investigation turned out to be a fairly thorough whitewashing of the facts, though the commission's final report did note that:

"Beginning in the late 1940's, the CIA began to study the properties of certain behavior-influencing drugs and how such drugs might be put to use in intelligence activities ... The drug program was part of a much larger CIA program to study possible means for controlling human behavior. Other studies explored the effects of radiation, electric shock, psychology, psychiatry, sociology, and harassment substances."

On April 30 of 1975, with Saigon on the verge of surrender, Ford ordered the evacuation of all remaining American 'civilian' personnel from Vietnam, virtually all of whom were intelligence agents. Also airlifted out were 237,000 rabidly anti-communist refugees, most of whom were resettled in the United States as yet another pro-fascist émigré group.

In September of the same year, two assassination attempts were made on Ford, both in California. Had either proven successful, Rockefeller would have assumed the presidency as the second consecutive man to hold that office who had been elected neither president nor vice president.

On December 6 of 1975, President Ford and Secretary of State Henry Kissinger paid a visit to President Suharto in Indonesia.

The next day, Indonesian forces armed with US-supplied weapons invaded the neighboring island of East Timor and began a bloodbath that would result in the deaths of some 200,000 inhabitants of the tiny nation.

In 1976, Ford was challenged for the Republican nomination by Ronald Reagan, though Gerry managed to fend off his opponent. He was defeated in the general election, however, despite having dropped Rockefeller in favor of Bob 'Viagra' Dole, thus beginning a quarter century in which the Republican Party presidential ticket included either Bob Dole or a George Bush. Turning the White House over to Jimmy Carter, Ford became a founding member of the American Enterprise Institute, an organization widely regarded as a CIA front.

Ford was reportedly in the midst of negotiating a co-presidency deal with Republican front-runner Ronald Reagan in 1980 before this unusual vice presidential arrangement leaked out in the press, killing the deal. George Bush was instead selected as the vice president/co-president.

Chapter 23

The Country Bumpkin, 1977-1981

James Earl Carter, Jr. was born in Plains, Georgia on October 1, 1924 to a staunchly segregationist and politically connected father. In 1941 he enrolled in Georgia Southwestern College, leaving after a year to attend the Georgia Institute of Technology, which he also left after a year.

Carter next attended the US Naval Academy at Annapolis, graduating in 1946. He was thereafter assigned to a naval submarine and soon began working under Admiral Hyman George Rickover – a high ranking naval intelligence officer who served as such for an unprecedented sixty-three years, thanks to a special act of Congress which exempted him from mandatory retirement.

In those post-war years, Rickover was the assistant director of operations on the Manhattan Project at Oak Ridge Nuclear Laboratory, and also served as chief of the Naval Reactors Branch of the US Atomic Energy Commission and head of the Nuclear Power Division of the US Navy. Young Jimmy Carter was to be trained by the best.

In 1953, Carter allegedly resigned from the navy to take over his father's store and peanut farm. Seven years later, he began his political career quite modestly with a seat on the local school board. Two years after that, he moved up to the Georgia state senate.

By 1966, Jimmy was ready to move up to the governor's office, but failed miserably in his first attempt to do so, taking third place in the Democratic primary. Four years later though, Carter was back with a vengeance, running a race-baiting campaign that garnered him a mere 10% of the state's black vote in the primary.

He was propelled into the governor's office nonetheless, and soon after started receiving a generous amount of national press coverage as a symbol of the 'New South' – though it was clearly the tactics of the old South that had gotten him elected. He was also widely touted as a symbol of a return to honesty in government, a particularly attractive quality in the wake of the breaking Watergate scandal.

Carter is said to have begun considering the presidency by the time he was halfway through his first gubernatorial term, and had formally announced his candidacy before that term expired. His obvious lack of experience in politics was portrayed as an asset: he was the outsider who was going to clean up Washington.

Running on this 'good old boy' platform, Carter narrowly defeated appointed incumbent Gerald Ford to become the 39th President of the United States. This victory was largely due, ironically enough, to the fact that Carter managed to capture 90% of the African-American vote nationwide.

The new president had made a number of promises while campaigning—albeit vague ones—virtually none of which was kept. He had vowed to slash the bloated defense budget and to cut back on overseas weapon sales, though both continued to steadily rise throughout his presidency – perhaps not surprising given Carter's long-standing support for the genocidal Vietnam War.

He had also pledged to reform the tax system to ease the burden on lower and middle-class Americans, but gave the idea nothing but lip service once in office. Carter left the economic policies of his Republican predecessors in place, and—unlike his Democratic predecessors—did not even go through the motions of proposing any new social welfare programs.

The country bumpkin soon found himself surrounded by scandal as well. Both his budget director, Bert Lance, and his United Nations Ambassador, Andrew Young, had to step down from office. Brother Billy was caught accepting a $220,000 payment from the nation of Libya, officially labeled a sponsor of terrorism by Carter's State Department.

The administration's Attorney General, Benjamin Civiletti, was accused of running interference for Billy, Chief of Staff Hamilton Jordan was accused of using cocaine, and Treasury Secretary G. William Miller was accused of graft. So much for cleaning up Washington.

America quickly grew disillusioned with the Carter presidency, particularly when an artificial oil shortage struck in 1979. The final straw came in November of that year when 53 Americans were taken hostage in Iran by students demanding the return of the hated Shah, who had been granted asylum to seek medical treatment in the United States.

In order to seal his fate, Reagan campaign officials—including possibly George Bush and campaign manager William Casey—met with Iranian representatives in Paris in October of 1980 to negotiate an arms deal in exchange for delaying the hostage release. With the hostages still being held and with no prospects for their release, and with John Anderson posing as a 'third party' candidate, Carter was soundly defeated in the 1980 election.

Chapter 24

The Acting President, 1981-1989

Ronald Wilson Reagan was born in Tampico, Illinois on February 6, 1911. Ronnie graduated from Eureka College and then went missing for a few years, eventually showing up in Des Moines, Iowa in 1936 as a sportscaster on a local radio station.

The next year, Reagan headed to Hollywood to begin an acting career that spanned the next twenty-five years (or more accurately, the next fifty-two years). He also quickly became active in the Screen Actors Guild, of which he became president, and spent a considerable amount of time working to purge suspected 'communists' from the unions.

Strangely enough, another man arrived in Hollywood at that same time, and he also quickly became involved with the unions, beginning with the extra's union. Once he had gained control of the unions, he went after the stars. His name was Bugsy Siegel, and he had been sent on behalf of the Lansky gang.

While living lavishly and consorting with some of the biggest names in Hollywood—including Jack Warner, Clark Gable, Cary Grant, Gary Cooper, Jean Harlow and childhood friend George

Raft—Siegel organized gambling operations in Los Angeles and set up a heroin and opium smuggling operation in Mexico and California.

Siegel also spent a considerable amount of time with Countess Dorothy Dendice Taylor DiFrasso. In 1939 he sailed with the Countess to pay a visit to the DiFrasso estate in Italy. While there, they entertained such guests as Benito Mussolini, Hermann Goering and Joseph Goebbels, then promptly returned to Hollywood to resume the co-opting of Tinseltown.

Mussolini was, it should be noted, reportedly a bitter foe of organized crime and had waged a highly publicized 'war' on the Mafia after assuming power. In truth though, Mussolini's war—like the Luciano gang's war and later that of Attorney General Robert Kennedy—was not intended to eliminate organized crime, but rather to eliminate the competition and bring the rackets firmly under the control of the state.

Il Duce had a close relationship with an associate of Luciano as well, future New York capo Vito Genovese. Vito fled the States for his native Italy in 1937 to avoid prosecution and remained a trusted ally of Mussolini throughout the war years. After the war, he worked for US Army Intelligence before being returned to America – allegedly to face trial, though the charges were dropped soon after his return and he shortly thereafter resumed his prominent position in the Lansky syndicate.

Just after World War II, William Casey—who had served in the OSS in Berlin during the war—began organizing the International Rescue Committee in New York, a front group created by US intelligence services to assist in relocating Nazi intelligence assets recruited through Project Paperclip.

Casey soon recruited Ronald Reagan to serve as the public relations man for the Crusade for Freedom, another intelligence front created to serve as a fundraising arm of the 'Rescue' Committee.

In 1954, Reagan began working with the General Electric Company hosting a television series and traveling the country delivering anti-communist and anti-union propaganda speeches to GE employees.

A decade later, Reagan appeared on national television delivering an impassioned plea to Americans to support the presidential candidacy of Barry Goldwater. Most voters though viewed Goldwater as a dangerous extremist. This was due in no small part to the ultra-reactionary campaign speeches being written for him by a young William Rehnquist.

Reagan, who until 1962 had been a registered Democrat, later enshrined the fascistic Rehnquist as Chief Justice of the Supreme Court. In 1966, the newly-Republican Reagan was elected governor of California, defeating Edmund Brown and avenging Richard Nixon's loss four years earlier. Reagan gained a second term in 1970.

Following his eight year run as governor, Reagan headed to Washington to join Rockefeller in pretending to look into abuses by the CIA. In 1976 he challenged Ford for the Republican presidential nomination but lost. Four years later he succeeded in gaining the nomination and chose George Bush as his running-mate.

Aided by the entry of 'third party' candidate John Anderson, and by a disillusioned public that largely stayed away from the polls, Reagan was elected the 40th President of the United States. Present at his inauguration was Licio Gelli, a friend of Reagan campaign manager Philip Guarino and the founder of the powerful P2 Lodge – a secretive pro-fascist organization with deep ties to the CIA, Italian intelligence and organized crime.

Appointed to Reagan's 'Kitchen Cabinet' was Peter Grace, who had brought Nazi gas warfare expert Otto Ambros into the United States. Colonel Albert Wedemeyer—who had accompanied Charles Lindbergh as an interpreter on tours of Nazi

munitions factories—was named as a special military advisor.
William Casey was appointed as the director of the CIA. He
had served under Nixon as the chairman of the SEC and as
Undersecretary of State, and had served Ford as a member of
the Foreign Intelligence Advisory Board.

The new administration quickly set about passing out tax
breaks to upper income individuals and corporations through the
Economic Recovery Act, while at the same time gutting spending
on job training, college loans, food and medical programs, dis-
ability payments, daycare centers and elderly centers.

The Reagan years also saw the relaxing of environmental and
safety standards and the deregulation of many industries.
Enforcement of antitrust laws was suspended, increases in military
spending were enacted and thousands of industrial jobs disappeared. Meanwhile, civil liberties and civil rights were severely
curtailed.

In 1983, Ronnie appointed Kissinger to head a national commission on Central America, where the administration was
actively supporting expatriate Nazi-trained death squads and various other forms of covert warfare. That same year, Ross Perot—
who would show up nine years later as an 'outsider'—was given a
position on the president's Foreign Intelligence Advisory Board.

Also that year, US troops under the command of H. Norman
Schwarzkopf were sent into Grenada following a coup that ousted
the US-controlled head of state. Though the invasion was billed as
a spontaneous response taken to protect the supposedly endan-
gered lives of American medical students on the island, the facts
indicate that the operation was planned at least two years in
advance.

In 1984, Reagan was challenged by the rather lackluster campaign of Walter Mondale and easily gained re-election. Shortly
after beginning his second term, he visited Germany's Bitburg

cemetery and laid a wreath honoring the memory of the Waffen SS. In 1986 he launched a surprise nighttime bombing raid of several Libyan cities, allegedly in response to the bombing of a West German disco.

The Reagan and Bush years were marked by an extraordinary number of overlapping scandals, including the aforementioned October Surprise, the Iran/Contra machinations, the Promis software scandal, the crack cocaine/Contra connection, the BCCI scandal, and the looting of America's Savings and Loans. The media expended considerable energy covering up and denying the numerous allegations, while at the same time marveling at the 'Teflon President' they had helped create.

Chapter 25

The Fortunate Son, 1989-1993

George Herbert Walker Bush was born on June 12, 1924 in Milton, Massachusetts. His father, Prescott Bush, had been an army intelligence agent in World War I. His paternal grandfather, Samuel P. Bush, had served as the chief of the Ordnance, Small Arms and Ammunitions Section of the War Industries Board, though he reportedly had no knowledge of firearms.

In 1942, Bush graduated from the exclusive Phillips Academy in Andover, Massachusetts. At the time, his father and his maternal grandfather, George Herbert 'Herb' Walker, were facing the possibility of being publicly exposed for collaborating with Nazi Germany through various subsidiaries of the Brown Brothers/Harriman Company.

In what was viewed by some as an effort to save the family honor, Bush enlisted in the US Navy and reportedly served as a pilot. As the story goes, Bush's plane was shot down over the Pacific but George managed to eject himself to safety. His crew though was not as fortunate: they went down with the plane.

Immediately upon his return in 1945, Bush married Barbara Pierce—a descendant of President Franklin Pierce—and enrolled at Yale University. In 1948 he graduated from Yale and headed off to Texas, ostensibly to work in the oil business. In 1953 he co-founded the Zapata Petroleum Corporation and the next year co-founded another entity – the Zapata Offshore Company.

Zapata's offshore facilities frequently functioned as intelligence fronts and, not coincidentally, developed a history of bidding on drilling contracts for Rockefeller's Standard Oil. In 1962, Bush became the Harris County Republican Party chairman; the same year, his father and William Casey co-founded the National Strategy Information Center, a New York based 'think tank.'

In 1964, Bush made his first run for elective office in the US Senate race and was soundly defeated. Two years later, he lowered his sights and ran for a House seat in an affluent, staunchly conservative district. With an assist from Richard Nixon, Bush won the seat and retained it two years later in the election that brought Nixon to the White House.

Bush stepped down in 1970 to make another run for the Senate, and to record yet another defeat. The unelectable Bush was nevertheless kept in the public eye with a series of high-profile appointments from Presidents Nixon and Ford, beginning with a stint as the US Ambassador to the United Nations in 1971.

He was next appointed as chairman of the Republican National Committee, from where he would publicly call on Nixon to step down. In 1974, Bush was appointed chief of the US Liaison Office in Peking, China. His final appointment was as Director of the Central Intelligence Agency. While serving as such, he warmly received as a guest a man named Manuel Noriega, whom he would again meet with in 1983.

In 1980, Bush was selected as the running-mate of Ronald Reagan and was swept into office as the vice president. Before assuming the office, he turned over his personal finances to a trusted friend, William S. Farish III. William had inherited a fortune at the age of four when both his father and grandfather had turned up dead following the public disclosure of the senior Farish as a Nazi collaborator.

The surviving Farish was known to play host to the Queen of England on her visits to the US, and to breed his champion thoroughbreds with those of the Royal Family. Bush himself has been reported by the *Los Angeles Times* to be a thirteenth cousin, twice removed, of Queen Elizabeth – and a direct descendant of King Henry III.

Eight years later, Bush was named the Republican nominee for president. He had not won an election on his own for twenty years, and even then it was only a local election. Part of his campaign strategy involved recruiting the same fascist émigré groups that had been organized during the Nixon campaigns.

A brief scandal emerged when several of Bush's connections in the Ethnic Outreach Division of the Republican National Committee were identified as former Nazis. There were actually many more on the roster with similar histories, though they avoided detection as the media obligingly looked away.

As a running-mate, Bush chose would-be boy-king Dan Quayle. This preposterous duo actually won the election—thanks to a weak opponent running an inept campaign—and in 1989 George Bush became the 41st President of the United States. Before the end of the year, he sent 24,000 US troops to Panama to serve an arrest warrant on his old friend Manuel Noriega.

In 1990, Haiti's freely elected leader, Jean Bertrand Aristide, was ousted by the US-trained Haitian military after serving just eight months and fascist rule was restored to the island. That same year, Germany—with the backing of the Bush Administration—encouraged the secession of Croatia from Yugoslavia, and Bosnia soon followed suit.

Germany formally recognized the new Croatian state immediately, even as it adopted the flag and symbolism of the puppet regime that had ruled during World War II. Throughout the decade, fascist underground movements active since the war began to spring to life in Lithuania, Hungary, Romania and through much of Western Europe.

On January 17, 1991, President Bush unleashed Operation Desert Storm on the people of Iraq, a massive military assault that was unprecedented in its ferocity. It was a dazzling display of US belligerence carried live—albeit sanitized—to the world, and demonstrated just how much killing power a decade of ridiculously bloated military budgets could buy.

The operation swelled Bush's popularity—along with that of the genocidal H. Norman Schwarzkopf, who had led the assault—but it was not enough to sustain his presidency. In 1992, Bush reverted to his old habit of losing national elections and relinquished control of the White House to Clinton.

Chapter 26

The Boy-King From Nowhere, 1993-2001

William Jefferson Blythe IV was born in Hope, Arkansas on August 19, 1946. He would later learn that his spooky father, allegedly a travelling salesman, had been secretly married several other times and had sired other offspring. Raised partly by his grandparents, young Billy was soon renamed William Clinton.

In 1963, Clinton was selected as one of two delegates to Boy's Nation from the state of Arkansas and sent to Washington, D.C. to meet President Kennedy in the Rose Garden. The next year he graduated from high school and headed back to Washington to attend prestigious Georgetown University, where he majored in international affairs and worked as an intern for the Senate Committee on Foreign Relations.

Four years later, Clinton graduated from Georgetown and headed off to England on a Rhodes Scholarship to attend the even more prestigious University of Oxford. After two years at Oxford, he headed back stateside to attend law school at Yale University. All in all, a pretty impressive academic résumé for a pauper from Hope, Arkansas.

On October 16, 1972, Clinton gave House Majority Leader Hale Boggs a ride to the airport to catch a flight to Alaska. The flight never made it, allegedly crashing enroute, though official reports claim the wreckage was never found. Boggs had served on the Warren Committee in 1964, when he was known as "LBJ's man in the House."

Since that time though, he had become one of the most vocal critics of the Committee's findings. Boggs had questioned the 'single bullet theory,' and had publicly accused Hoover's FBI of running a massive spying and wiretapping operation directed against members of the US Congress to blackmail them into accepting the findings in the Warren Report.

In 1973, Bill graduated from Yale and headed to Fayetteville, Arkansas to teach at the University of Arkansas Law School. Hillary Rodham, his soon-to-be wife who had also just graduated from law school, soon thereafter joined a congressional team pretending to investigate the Watergate scandal.

Clinton made his first run for public office in 1974, vying for a seat in the House of Representatives, but lost. He had better luck two years later when he was elected the state's attorney general. Of course it was much easier to win that election, given that nobody bothered to oppose the thirty-year-old political neophyte. Nothing unusual about that.

After a brief stint as attorney general, Clinton made a run for the governor's office in 1978 and won. He took office the next year at the wise old age of thirty-two. One of his biggest successes as governor was his highway program, improving what were some of the worst roads in the country – entirely unsuitable for, say, transporting large quantities of drugs and weapons.

After just two years in office, Clinton was defeated in his bid for re-election. His decline in popularity was due partially to his wholehearted support during his first term of a plan by President

Carter to house 18,000 anti-Castro Cuban refugees at an old US
Army post near Fort Smith, Arkansas.

Clinton was back in the race in 1982 with a new strategy – pan-
dering for the black vote. The strategy worked and Clinton
regained the governorship with a full 95% of the state's sizable
African-American vote. Shortly after his inauguration, Mena,
Arkansas became a major transshipment point for the illegal
Contra arming and funding operation.

In 1984, Clinton once again gained re-election and the Mena
operations were expanded to include a covert training camp for
Contra guerrillas. The governor's newly-created Arkansas
Development Finance Authority made its first loan in 1985 to a
company calling itself Park on Meter, Inc. The entity was headed
by 'Skeeter' Ward, a brother-in-law of Web Hubbell.

Hubbell, who was at the time working with Hillary Clinton at
the Rose Law Firm, and who would later serve as Clinton's
Assistant Attorney General, had assured the loan to Park on
Meter. Some investigators would later allege that the business
entity was under covert contract to manufacture components of
chemical and biological weapons intended for use by the Contras.

In 1986, Clinton was once again elected governor, this time for
a four year term, and became the chairman of the National
Governor's Association. Four years later he was re-elected yet
again, and also became the head of the Democratic Leadership
Council. Halfway through this final term, Clinton abandoned a
campaign promise to serve out his term and tossed his hat in the
presidential ring.

Not long into his presidential campaign, rumors of Contra
operations at Mena began flying, prompting *Time* magazine to
run a piece on April 15 entitled "Anatomy of a Smear," denounc-
ing the rumors as unfounded and effectively preempting any
exposés of the scandal. With all challengers except the absurd

Jerry Brown dropping out of the race, Clinton easily clinched the Democratic nomination.

Pamela Churchill Harriman, former wife of both Randolph Churchill and Averell Harriman, held a one-day fund raiser at her Middleburg, Virginia estate and collected $3 million for Clinton's campaign – which focused on domestic policy, promising a range of social reforms and new discretionary spending.

Meanwhile, at the Republican Convention, rabid right-wingers held the stage, splintering the party faithful. Elsewhere, 'outsider' H. Ross Perot had launched an independent candidacy which proved to do more than merely split the Republican vote; by summer he was leading both major party candidates in the polls, which clearly wasn't part of the plan.

Perot therefore dropped out of the race in July, losing much of his prior support. He still had enough though to drain votes away from Bush when he re-entered the race in October. Clinton ultimately won the three-way race with just 43% of the vote and took office in 1993 as the 42nd President of the United States.

Once in office, Clinton balked on the gays in the military issue and on national healthcare and instead passed an anti-crime bill that liberalized the use of the death penalty and gave the states money to hire 100,000 additional police officers; the use of the death penalty and incarceration rates soon began to skyrocket.

Clinton also greatly increased foreign arms sales and the privatization of America's prisons. An anti-terrorism bill was passed providing more money to fight the phantom specter of terrorism and making it easier to deport foreigners. The administration also authorized covert actions in Haiti, doubled the number of troops deployed in Somalia, and sent troops in to occupy Bosnia, while continuing the genocidal bombing and sanctions campaign against Iraq.

Bombs were also lobbed at the Sudan, Afghanistan and Yugoslavia, while the Rwandan genocide was completely ignored. 'Free' trade legislation was wholeheartedly supported and passed, including NAFTA in 1993 and GATT in a special lame duck session of Congress after the 1994 elections.

That same year, the CIA opened a new base in Albania, beginning the machinations that would lead to the aerial bombardment of Yugoslavia five years later. In September of 2000, with Clinton's second term coming to an end, Elliot Roosevelt, Jr.—grandson of FDR—lent his endorsement to the campaign of George W. Bush. In November, just days before the election, 'outsider' Ross Perot also endorsed the chosen son. And so it goes.

PART III

Further Adventures in the Politics of Illusion

The Fascist State organizes the nation, but leaves a sufficient margin of liberty to the individual; the latter is deprived of all useless and possibly harmful freedom, but retains what is essential; the deciding power in this question cannot be the individual, but the State alone.

Benito Mussolini, 1932

Chapter 27

A Slice of Hidden History

"We are also being told, as we were to justify the genocidal war with Iraq, that Serbia's leader—Slobodan Milosevic—is evil incarnate, the heir apparent to Adolph Hitler. From this we are to deduce that Milosevic is a madman bent on global imperialism and genocidal actions of horrendous proportions, and with the resources to achieve his goals. This analogy could not possibly be any more absurd ...

"There is, however, a chilling parallel with Hitler that has gone unmentioned in the US press. In 1938, Nazi Germany invaded Czechoslovakia for the allegedly purely humanitarian aim of ending ethnic violence in the Sudenten region of the country. Conveniently left out of this justification was the fact that the Nazis had actively encouraged an uprising in that area for the express purpose of using the repression of that movement by Czech forces as a pretext for the military intervention. We might also note here that Nazi Germany was the last imperialist power to rain bombs down upon the Serbian capital of Belgrade."

Those are the words that I wrote in April of 1999 as part of an angry diatribe deploring the bombing of Yugoslavia, which later became the epilogue of my first book, *Derailing Democracy*. It has recently been brought to my attention that the final statement made in that passage is untrue. As it turns out, the last imperialist power to drop bombs on Belgrade prior to the ones dropped last year was not in fact Nazi Germany – but was none other than the United States of America.

Of course, you won't find that in any English language text-books or histories of the war, which is why when I wrote those words a year-and-a-half ago, I believed them to be the truth. It seems that in Belgrade, though, they remember the war a little differently than we do. I found that out when I recently received the following correspondence from Dragan Ambrozic, a Serbian citizen and resident of Belgrade:

> "I just found one small mistake—on page 208 you mention that, before NATO bombing campaign in 1999, the last imperialist power to bomb Belgrade was Nazi Germany (6th of April 1941). Not quite true—Allied Air Force did the heaviest bombing on Belgrade in World War 2, on Orthodox Easter 1944 (and on few more occasions during 1944). This is not something anybody is keen on remembering, and I doubt you will find much about it even in more serious histories of that period, but my father (b. 1935) has a lot of recollections of that event, and quite a few books on the subject. Seems that joint American-British Air Force efforts were directed on cutting away the southern group of German Armies (Group "E") from pulling out of Greece and Balkans. Being the biggest junction, Belgrade was an obvious target, but no one is explaining how come that the strategy applied in bombing of this city was apparently same as the one applied to any German city—with much heavier civilian losses reported then during the original Nazi air attack. Just to remind that Tito's

partisans were accepted in 1943 by Allies as legitimate part of anti-fascist coalition, and even before this, it was clear that there was anti-nazi uprising in Yugoslavia, so this brutal bombing stays as a mystery."

Naturally intrigued by this, I inquired as to whether there were any English language accounts of these long-forgotten (or perhaps never recorded) events. Alas, my source was unable to locate any. He was able to locate a number of Serbian language versions though, which he was gracious enough to summarize for me.

In order to put these bombings in some kind of historical context, I have taken the information that I was provided and combined it with other events that were occurring at the time in the European theater of the war. We begin on March 25, 1944, a significant date in that, as previously noted, it marked the first time that Red Army troops of the Soviet Union stood on a portion of their pre-war western border since the massive invasion by Nazi Germany launched on June 22, 1941.

Though the US had joined the war effort some six months after the invasion, there remained only one front in Europe of any significance: the Eastern Front. Despite repeated pleas by Stalin to the Western powers to open up a second front, and despite repeated promises from Churchill and Roosevelt to do so, the Red Army had stood virtually alone against the scourge of European fascism for nearly three years, at a cost of millions of lives.

Now Soviet forces were approaching the Balkans from Romania and the Ukraine, and a couple of weeks later—on April 8—the Soviets launched a Crimean offensive aimed at reclaiming that region from German occupation. On this very same day, the first Allied bombs fell on Belgrade. This first attack was rather small, with minimal damage, and appeared to witnesses to be something of a test bombing.

In any case, as my corespondent notes, "Serbians considered themselves as an Allied nation under occupation, so the initial Anglo-American bombings took everybody by surprise." As well they should have. Five days later, on April 13, Allied bombs again fell on Belgrade, followed two days later by yet another attack on the city. Then, on April 16—Orthodox Easter—"all hell broke loose."

On that day and the next, over 700 Allied planes dumped an untold amount of ordnance on the besieged city, wreaking massive destruction. Some of the targets were exclusively civilian, with entire city blocks wiped out. Another target was the Staro Sajmiste concentration camp, which was almost completely destroyed, possibly to destroy evidence of Nazi atrocities or of Western complicity in the setting up of the forced labor camps.

The method of bombing appeared to be something new, perhaps experimental. The bombs were reportedly connected into clusters with chains, described by my source as a "non-selective way of bombing." The result was that "Civilians just doesn't have any chance to escape, when exposed to this massive destruction style bombing, so there were hardly any survivors in the houses that were hit."

According to the official estimates released by the government of occupation, there were 1,360 resultant casualties—85% of them civilian—though everyone who was there knows this figure to be ridiculously low. As Dragan notes, the Nazi command "didn't bother very much to go through the ruined buildings and count dead Serbians." He also notes that corpses were still being found among the rubble "a full year or two after the final liberation of Belgrade."

The Allied bombers returned on April 21, when a fleet of approximately one hundred planes unloaded on the city of Zemun, lying just across the Sava River and now an integral part of the city of Belgrade. They returned to Zemun on April 23 and 24, and to Belgrade itself on April 25. Reports of the damage caused by these raids are rather sketchy as there was essentially no functioning government at the time.

The next Allied attack, on May 7, was targeted at the bridge to Pancevo, a main road leading to and from neighboring Romania. Dragan reports: "Bearing in mind that Soviet forces were coming from that direction, and no Germans were escaping that way—it looks strange." To say the least.

Nevertheless, my source was quick to give the US the benefit of the doubt, noting that: "who can tell military logic from foreign politics when the bombing actually starts." Less charitable minds might wonder whether the attack was deliberately intended to hold the Red Army at bay and provide cover for the retreating Nazis, which clearly was the result of the bombing, if not the intent.

As the Soviets continued their westward advance, another enormous load of bombs was dropped on Belgrade on May 18. This attack differed from the previous ones in that the Allies were now dropping massive 1,500 kilogram bombs, along with napalm and what were described as "magnetic bombs" intended to "stop traffic on the Danube and Sava rivers" (though what is meant by this is not entirely clear).

This was the last large-scale bombing attack on Belgrade during the war years, although smaller attacks continued throughout the summer and autumn of 1944. The first of these occurred on June 6, a day remembered by Americans as D-Day. As Eisenhower's men were storming the beaches of Normandy, US bombs again fell on the capital city of a US ally. And while Belgrade was being repeatedly pummeled with bombs through the months of April and May, so too were large swaths of France being carpet-bombed.

Just three days after D-Day, the Red Army invaded Finland and began pounding the Mannerheim Line, alleged to be the most impregnable in the world. It proved to be no match for the Soviet forces however, and the entire Nazi line from Finland to the Baltics was soon being pushed back. It was abundantly clear to everyone by this time that the German and Axis forces were not going to be able to hold back the Red Army, which on June 23 began a major offensive into Belarussia, the last Soviet territory still under Nazi occupation.

About this same time, the British War Cabinet ruled that the UN War Crimes Commission should be prohibited from collecting information about the murder of Axis nationals. This occurred, by coincidence or otherwise, at precisely the time that mass gassings of Hungarian Jews were underway at the hands of Axis forces. As a direct result of the British ruling, the perpetrators of these crimes against humanity would never be held accountable for their actions.

In July, the Bretton Woods conference was held, leading to the creation of the International Monetary Fund and the World Bank, which would thenceforth be utilized to promote global fascism. Dean Acheson, a former lawyer for Standard Oil, argued success-fully for the retention of the Bank for International Settlements, an entity created in 1930 by a coalition of international bankers that was used to 'legalize' the looting of Europe by Nazi Germany and for laundering the proceeds.

The bank's first president was Gates McGarrah, a Rockefeller banker and the grandfather of future CIA Director Richard Helms. Hjalmar Schacht played a prominent role in setting up the BIS, as did, of course, John Foster Dulles. The first chronicler of the bank was none other than Eleanor Lansing Dulles, and one of its first directors was Hermann Schmitz – the chairman of I.G. Farben and a close associate of William S. Farish.

Also in July, the Soviets liberated the first Nazi death camp at
Majdanek. The Soviet press carried detailed coverage, including
grisly photographic documentation of gas chambers, crematoria
and piles of human bones. Western press reports, on the other
hand, were sketchy at best and delivered with a healthy dose of
skepticism; needless to say, no photographic evidence was presented. Meanwhile, on July 8, Belgrade was again subjected to an
Allied bombing attack.

On July 17, a victory celebration was held in Moscow in honor
of the fact that the Red Army had by that time reclaimed all of the
pre-war borders of the Soviet Union. The Soviets though had two
more goals in mind: the destruction of the Nazi war machine and
the creation of a buffer zone for protection against future invasions. In pursuit of these objectives, Red Army forces had already
penetrated deep into Poland and Lithuania.

Three days later, a bomb blast nearly claimed the life of Adolf
Hitler, though he escaped with minor injuries, thereby thwarting a
plan to give the Reich a quick facelift and seek a negotiated peace
with the West. The SS quickly seized all power and launched a
brutal purge that saw seven thousand arrests and nearly five thousand executions before it was over. By this time, back-up plans
were well underway to establish safe retreats for the Nazi elite,
facing certain defeat from the East; Martin Bormann and
Hermann Schmitz were instrumental in coordinating these plans.

To Hjalmar Schacht fell the duty of arranging the movement of
looted Nazi treasure out of Europe and the expatriation of industrial assets. Otto Skorzeny, known as 'Hitler's favorite commando,' was given responsibility for the movement of SS
personnel. Identified as desirable destinations for émigré Nazi
communities were Argentina, Paraguay, South Africa, Indonesia
and Egypt, the last of which would become the destination for
some of Germany's top biological and chemical warfare special-

ists, courtesy of Allen Dulles and British intelligence asset Miles Copeland, working in conjunction with Otto Skorzeny.

A network of 'rat lines' was already being established leading from various parts of Germany to the Bavarian city of Memmingen, then on to Rome with the collusion of the Vatican, and finally by sea to a number of budding Nazi colonies. The Gehlen Organization—an enormous Nazi intelligence network responsible for a plethora of crimes against humanity committed on the Eastern Front, but which was nevertheless recruited *in toto* by US intelligence services—would provide cover for the operation, which later became known as Odessa. The fledgling CIA, along with various other interwoven US intelligence entities, would oversee the entire sordid affair.

Five days after the assassination attempt on Hitler, the Allies broke out of their beachhead to form the Western Front and began quickly moving across France. The Red Army was at the time just 400 miles from Berlin, but with 80% of Germany's remaining troops standing in their path. By mid-August, the first US divisions were crossing the Seine River in France, and two new Soviet thrusts had begun into Eastern Europe. Time was quickly running out for the Third Reich.

In early September, Estonia and Bulgaria both fell to the Soviets, and Red Army troops joined with Tito's Partisans in a drive designed to trap Axis troops in Bulgaria and Greece. The Western Allies were meanwhile approaching the German border, having advanced 350 miles in just a few weeks. On September 11, the first US advance patrols began slipping across the border, the regular forces having come to a halt.

On that very same day, Roosevelt and Churchill met in Quebec for what was dubbed the Octagon Conference, presumably to discuss the Allied end-game strategy. Despite the fact that the USSR had been almost single-handedly carrying the war effort in Europe, Stalin was excluded from the conference.

Also in September, the Soviet Union filed a formal protest charging British intelligence services with actively recruiting from among Axis prisoners-of-war to assemble anti-communist paramilitary units to fight the USSR. Though UK officials predictably feigned outrage, the charges were certainly not without merit. US intelligence services would play an even larger role in fashioning rabidly fascist, paramilitary 'stay behind' cells to disrupt the workings of the post-war European governments should they lean even slightly to the left.

The Octagon Conference concluded on September 16, and three days later Finland surrendered to the Red Army. On October 9 another conference began – the Moscow Conference, hosted by Josef Stalin. Churchill attended to represent the UK, and Nazi collaborator Averell Harriman was sent to represent the US, along with John Foster Dulles. While the conference was being held, Latvia and Lithuania fell to the Red Army and Yugoslavia was liberated by a combination of Red Army forces and Partisans. The war, in Belgrade at least, was over.

The city and its people though had paid a heavy price. Thirty-six percent of the city's buildings had been destroyed and 50,000 people were missing and presumed dead as a result of three major events: the Nazi bombing in 1941, the Allied bombing in 1944, and the street fighting during the liberation of the city. As Dragan notes: "The huge portion definitely died during Allied bombing campaign in Spring 1944, but we will never know even the close number..."

I would hope that it would be clear to most readers by this time that the Allied bombing of Belgrade was not an anomalous act, but was rather part of a pattern of actions that collectively constituted what can only be described as a covert war against the

Soviet Union carried out under the cover of a false war being waged against Germany.

The nation of Yugoslavia had fallen to the Axis in 1941, the people sold out by their fascist leaders. Prince Paul was summoned to Germany in February for the proposal of an alliance – an alliance to which the people of Yugoslavia were fiercely opposed. Upon his return, the prince pushed a German coup plan through his cabinet on March 20, and four days later the nation formally signed an agreement with the Axis in Vienna.

The people, however, rejected the pact and the army seized power, defying the actions of the heads of state. On April 4, the USSR and Yugoslavia signed a treaty of friendship. Nazi troops promptly invaded and began ruthlessly bombing Belgrade. The city fell a week later, and a few days after that, the main Yugoslavian armies collapsed.

On April 17, a capitulation was signed in Belgrade carving up the Balkans, though partisans led by Tito continued throughout the war to actively resist occupation. Interestingly enough, Wild Bill Donovan had paid a visit to Belgrade just hours before Nazi stormtroopers began streaming across the border. Strange how that works.

Before closing, I should note that on September 3, 1944, Allied bombs dropped on Belgrade for the final time, the attack targeted specifically at the bridge over the Sava River. Almost fifty-five years later, the bombs would begin falling again, this time with a ferocity the region had not seen even in the darkest days of World War II.

Chapter 28

Lies My Psychology Professors Taught Me

[New] technologies are conditioning a growing segment of the society to regard all deviance as sickness and to accept increasingly narrow standards of acceptable behavior as scientifically normative ... Together the new programs and technologies are part of a burgeoning establishment involving welfare institutions, universities, hospitals, the drug industry, government at all levels, and organized psychiatry (itself in large part a creation of government) ... The ideal, in the view of the behaviorists, is the paranoid's dream, a method so smooth that no one will know his behavior is being manipulated and against which no resistance is therefore possible ... There is no longer a set of impositions which he can regard as unjust or capricious and against which he can dream of rebelling. To entertain such dreams would be madness. Gradually, even the ability to imagine alternatives begins to fade. This is, after all, not only the best of all possible worlds; it is the only one.
                    Peter Schrag *Mind Control*, Pantheon, 1978

I have a degree in psychology from UCLA. I don't know exactly where it is, though I'm sure it's safely filed away somewhere. It's not really worth much though. I don't mean that it doesn't have much value in the job market, though that is surely the case. No, it isn't worth much because it was awarded to me on the supposition that I had gained a substantial level of knowledge about the field of psychology, which in hindsight was clearly a faulty premise.

It's not that I didn't try to learn. I actually did a very good job of regurgitating back the information that was presented to me, even graduating with honors. No, the problem was that—despite the exalted reputation of the UCLA psychology department—none of my professors seemed to be particularly interested in teaching me what psychology is really about.

I have a much better understanding now, though I had to fill in many of the gaps in my education on my own. Doing so, by the way, took considerably less time than the four years I spent being spoon-fed pseudo-knowledge at college. Society doesn't place any value on the acquisition of such knowledge however, so I don't have any kind of degree for my post-college education. Nevertheless, I thought I'd pass along some of the information that I wasn't formally taught, for whatever it's worth.

One thing I *was* taught was that John Watson is a much revered figure in the field of psychology, considered the father of 'behaviorism.' Watson, who began his career in 1908 as a professor of psychology and the director of the psychological laboratory at Johns Hopkins University, was perhaps most notable for venturing into the field of infant study in 1918 – at the time a largely unexplored area of research.

Watson conditioned a fear response in an infant identified only as 'Little Albert,' afterwards triumphantly declaring that "men are built, not born." Ten years later, Watson penned what was at the time considered the bible of child-rearing, *Psychological Care of Infant and Child*, assuming the mantle that would later be worn by Dr. Spock.

Unfortunately, there are a couple of elements of this story that seem to have been omitted from my textbooks, one of which is that Little Albert was not just some random infant; he was, in fact, the illegitimate son of the good doctor himself. And how did the reigning expert on childcare fare as a father? Not too well, it seems: Albert Watson was so traumatized by his upbringing at the hands of his father that he committed suicide shortly after reaching adulthood.

Watson had long since left his position at Johns Hopkins amidst a nasty divorce from his first wife, presumably precipitated by her displeasure with the revelation that Watson's experiments had included impregnating his nurse and torturing their resultant offspring.

In 1921, Watson headed for Madison Avenue where he put the behavior modification expertise he had acquired by traumatizing infants to work on a society-wide level, ushering in the era of modern propaganda (oops, I meant to say advertising). Along the way, he would find US intelligence services to be an excellent source of funding, as would all the characters in this sordid tale.

Following closely in the footsteps of Dr. Watson was B.F. Skinner, the other revered figure in the behaviorist school of psychology. Skinner—who had received a defense grant during World War II to study the training of pigeons for use as part of an early missile guidance system (I don't just make this shit up)—invented what he termed the 'Air Crib' in 1945, which was essentially a sensory deprivation chamber built specifically for infants.

Like Watson, he used his own child as a human guinea pig, raising her in the thermostatically controlled, sound-proof isolation chamber for the first two years of her life, cut off from human contact. Skinner ultimately followed a bit too closely in the footsteps of his mentor; Debby Skinner, like Albert Watson, committed suicide in her twenties.

In 1948, Skinner joined the faculty of Harvard, putting him in the company of such luminaries as Dr. Martin Orne, the head of the Office of Naval Research's Committee on Hypnosis and later a prominent member of the False Memory Syndrome Foundation. Skinner and Orne—as well as numerous others at Harvard, including Timothy Leary and Richard Alpert—received heavy funding from both the CIA and the US Army.

In 1971, Skinner published an unabashedly fascistic diatribe entitled *Beyond Freedom and Dignity*, advocating a dystopian society in which freedom and dignity were outmoded concepts. It earned him a cover story in *Time* magazine and the honor of having his work named the most important book of the year by the *New York Times*.

Also on board at Harvard at the time was Dr. Henry Murray, overseeing the work of Leary's Psychedelic Drug Research Program and various other CIA-funded projects. So deified was this man during my years at UCLA that an entire undergraduate course focused almost exclusively on his supposedly brilliant work. Yet during that course, no mention was ever made of the fact that Murray was a fully owned asset of the intelligence community. Recruited during World War II by none other than Wild Bill Donovan, Murray was put to work running the Personality Assessments section of the OSS.

Murray's best known contribution to the field of personality assessment—the Thematic Apperception Test (TAT)—was in fact developed as a tool of the US military/intelligence complex. After the war, Murray was one of the key players in the CIA's MK-ULTRA projects, studying various methods of achieving control of the human mind. One of his best research subjects during his days at Harvard was a young undergraduate by the name of Theodore Kaczynski.

Perhaps even more revered than Murray was Dr. Louis Jolyon West, the head of the UCLA Psychiatry Department and the director of the prestigious UCLA Neuropsychiatric Institute. Dr. West was another prominent participant in the MK-ULTRA program who would eventually wind up on the board of the False Memory Syndrome Foundation. His work with the military/intelligence community began at least as far back as 1958, when he conducted studies funded by the US Air Force in surviving torture as a prisoner-of-war.

If you're wondering how it is possible to study the conditioning of soldiers to survive torture without *inflicting* that very same torture in the process, the answer is simple: it isn't. A few years later, West achieved a moment of fame when he injected a beloved elephant at the Oklahoma City Zoo with a massive 300,00 microgram dose of LSD to observe how it would react; Tusko's reaction was to promptly drop dead.

In 1964, West was called upon to evaluate the 'mental state' of a man by the name of Jack Ruby, at the time being held pending trial for the murder of Lee Harvey Oswald. West quickly determined that Ruby was delusional, based on his obviously absurd belief that there was some sort of fascist conspiracy behind the assassination of President Kennedy. Dr. Jolly, as he was known to colleagues, ordered Ruby drugged with 'happy pills.' Ruby subsequently died of cancer, which he maintained he had been deliberately infected with. Having finished up that assignment, the doctor soon after found himself a crash-pad in the Haight where he could 'observe' the acid subculture in its native environment by drugging unwitting 'subjects.'

West is probably most notorious for proposing in 1972 to then California Governor Ronald Reagan the creation of the Center for the Study and Reduction of Violence, to be built on a remote abandoned missile test site in the Santa Monica Mountains. Among his earliest recruits were Leonard Rubenstein—formerly a top aide to Dr. David Ewen Cameron—as well as two South American doctors who had also worked for Cameron – one to run the shock room and the other to run the psychosurgery suite. At the time, the two were employed at 'detention centers' in Paraguay and Chile, which is a nice way of saying that they were working at torture/interrogation centers run by Nazi exile communities.

Also recruited by West was Dr. Frank Ervin, one of a trio of Harvard psychosurgeons who had not long before proposed lobotomy as the solution to urban 'rioting'. The center was to work in conjunction with California law enforcement and had secured large grants from the US Law Enforcement Assistance Administration and the National Institute of Mental Health (these two organizations had forged a close alliance in 1970 with the encouragement of the Nixon Administration, with both of them heavily involved in funding MK-ULTRA projects). There were to be psychologists, physicians and sociologists on board—mostly recruited from among West's disciples at the Neuropsychiatric Institute—as well as lawyers, police officers, probation officers and clergymen.

The goal of the center was to identify 'predelinquents' and treat them before their 'deviance' and supposed propensity for violence could be manifest. The team believed that predelinquents could be identified on the basis of several factors: socioeconomic status (poor), age (young), ethnicity (black), and sex (males). Treatments under consideration included electroshock, chemical castration, experimental drug therapy, and psychosurgery – better known as lobotomy (the 'surgical' destruction of the frontal lobes of the brain).

Lobotomy was, curiously enough, developed in fascist Portugal in 1935 by Dr. Egaz Moniz as a tool of social control. It was introduced to America the following year by James Watts and Walter Freeman, the latter of whom would later boast of having personally performed over 4,000 lobotomies in the United States, for all of the following 'conditions': apprehension, anxiety, depression, compulsions, obsessions, drug addiction, and sexual deviance.

By the post-war years, lobotomy was big business, warmly embraced by the Veteran's Administration and heartily recommended for vets suffering from combat-related 'disorders.' Moniz's procedure did not prove too popular with his patients however. In 1939 he was shot and partially paralyzed by a former patient. Sixteen years later, another former patient finished the job, beating Nobel laureate Moniz to death.

Electro-shock therapy was likewise an import from fascist Europe, developed by Ugo Cerletti in Mussolini's Italy in 1938. Appropriately enough, this 'medical advance' was based on Cerletti's observation of cattle being jolted into submission as they were being led to slaughter. Another form of shock therapy— insulin shock—was introduced by Manfred Sakel in fascist Austria (Sakel also practiced in Berlin) just a few years earlier.

One name that never came up in my years at UCLA was that of the aforementioned Dr. David Ewen Cameron. Considering that Cameron is probably the most honored North American psychiatrist of the last half-century, this appears in retrospect a rather remarkable omission. During his career, Cameron founded the Canadian Mental Health Association and served as chairman of the Canadian Scientific Planning Committee, president of the American Psychiatric Association, president of the Canadian Psychiatric Association, and the first president of the World Association of Psychiatrists. He was also the psychiatrist most thoroughly co-opted by US intelligence services in all of North America.

His intelligence career began at least as early as 1941, when he was sent by Allen Dulles to England on behalf of the OSS to 'ascertain the state of mind' of Rudolph Hess, Hitler's right-hand man who had supposedly 'defected' to the UK. Cameron was during this time a member of the Military Mobilization Committee of the American Psychiatric Association, in which capacity he also worked closely with Dulles.

By 1943, Cameron had founded the Allan Memorial Institute in Montreal with a generous grant from (where else?) the Rockefeller Foundation. The institute continued to receive lavish support from the Rockefellers for at least the next decade, as well as receiving the generous support of the CIA through various funding conduits.

In 1946, Cameron helped craft the Nuremberg Code on medical research, setting ethical guidelines for human research that were perhaps nowhere more flagrantly ignored than at his own Institute. Cameron's MK-ULTRA operation conducted what were undoubtedly among the most appalling of the CIA-funded mind control experiments (those that are well documented, anyway), utilizing what he euphemistically termed 'depatterning' and 'psychic driving.'

During the 'depatterning' phase, the objective was to completely obliterate the existing personality. This was done by restraining the victims (oops, I meant patients) for weeks on end and subjecting them to massive doses of drugs and repeated electroshock treatments. Cameron preferred the Page-Russell electroshock technique—controversial even among the shock docs of the time—which employed six consecutive shocks rather than just one big jolt. This wasn't quite enough for Cameron though, so he cranked up the power to as much as twenty times the normal strength, and administered the 'treatment' two or three times a day. Concurrently given three times a day were drug cocktails containing every combination of incapacitating and mind-altering drug imaginable.

Following some two months of this medical torture, patients were then subjected to 'psychic driving,' during which they were again incapacitated by drugs—including curare, a paralyzing agent which can be lethal—while taped messages were played continuously through speakers placed in pillows or in helmets the unfortunate victims were forced to wear. This also went on for weeks on end, with the subjects remaining drug-addled throughout the process. Cameron experimented with other techniques as well, including psychosurgery and the extensive use of LSD; one woman was kept locked in a small box for thirty-five consecutive days.

In 1960, Cameron was asked by Allen Dulles to evaluate the mental state of U-2 pilot Francis Gary Powers upon his return from the Soviet Union. So impressed was Dulles with Cameron's assessment of Powers that he next had him draft a psychological profile of Patrice Lumumba—the first Prime Minister of the newly independent Congo—to determine what the most efficient means of assassinating him might be.

Premier spymaster William Buckley took the agency's file on Lumumba to Montreal for Cameron's review; by January of the following year, Lumumba was dead, his body dissolved in acid after enduring a month of barbaric torture. As for Buckley, he would later be present at both the attempted assassination of Pope John Paul and the successful assassination of Egyptian President Anwar Sadat, whose security forces he had personally trained.

Working with Cameron on his experiments—some of which are believed by some researchers to have been terminal—were Leonard Rubenstein, an Englishman and former member of the British Army's Royal Signal Corp, and Jan Zielinski, a Polish-born engineer who knew only limited English and rarely spoke. These two built a 'grid room' and an isolation chamber in the basement of Allan Memorial and were given unlimited access to patients, despite the fact that neither had any formal medical training or qualifications. Also on board was Dr. Hassam Azima—rumored to be a blood relative of the US-installed Shah of Iran—and Dr. Wilder Penfield, a prominent neurologist.

Penfield was one of the pioneers in the field of electromagnetic control of the brain in the 1960's. Most prominent in this area of research was Dr. Jose M.R. Delgado, who made the front page of the *New York Times* when one of his remote-controlled brain implants stopped a charging bull dead in its tracks. Delgado— who brought his ideas here from fascist Spain and was heavily funded by the CIA—was an open advocate of a psychologically controlled, totalitarian society. Probably nowhere can the true nature of psychology be better discerned than from the words of this Dr. Strangelove.

In his Orwellian titled book, *Physical Control of the Mind: Toward a Psychocivilized Society*, Delgado wrote that "the integration of neurophysiological and psychological principles [would lead] to a more intelligent education, starting from the moment of birth and continuing throughout life, with the preconceived plan of escaping from the blind forces of chance and of influencing cerebral mechanisms and mental structure in order to create a future man with greater personal freedom and originality, a member of a psychocivilized society, happier, less destructive, and better balanced than present man."

He supported the mass drugging of America with "tranquilizers, energizers, and other psychoactive drugs," which he claimed were "highly beneficial both for patients and for relatively normal persons who need pharmacological help to cope with the pressures of civilized life." Lobotomy was proposed as the answer to crime: "the possibility of surgical rehabilitation of criminals has been considered by several scientists as more humane, more promising, and less damaging for the individual than his incarceration for life."

Delgado also made the rather remarkable observation that: "In some old plantations slaves behaved very well, worked hard, were submissive to their masters, and were probably happier than some of the free blacks in modern ghettos." Ahh, the good old days. Delgado next noted that: "In several dictatorial countries the general population is skillful, productive, well behaved, and perhaps as happy as those in more democratic societies."

Five years after penning his manifesto, Delgado appeared before the US Congress and proclaimed: "We need a program of psychosurgery for political control of our society. The purpose is physical control of the mind. Everyone who deviates from the given norm can be surgically mutilated ... The individual may think that the most important reality is his own existence, but this is only his personal point of view. This lacks historical perspective ... Man does not have the right to develop his own mind." Such talk earned Delgado funding from the Office of Naval Research, the Air Force Aero-Medical Research Laboratory, and the Public Health Foundation of Boston.

* * * * * * * * * * * * * * * * * * * *

What has been covered here barely scratches the surface of the lies and omissions that characterized my education in the field of psychology. There is considerably more that could be said on the subject. I could mention, for instance, that two of the most widely referenced psychological studies—Philip Zimbardo's Stanford Prison experiment and Stanley Milgram's obedience studies—were funded by, and performed at the request of, US military and intelligence services.

I could also mention that the National Institute of Mental Health (NIMH)—created in 1946 by the congressional National

Mental Health Act—was borne of the combined efforts of Robert H. Felix (head of the military's Division of Mental Hygiene during World War II), General Lewis Hershey (director of the Selective Service System), and the chief psychiatrists of the Army and the Navy. In fact, the *Diagnostic and Statistical Manual of Mental Disorders*—the bible of modern psychiatry—was also an invention of the military/intelligence complex, developed during World War II by Brigadier General William Menninger to codify 'deviant' behavior, and later institutionalized by the APA.

And of course I would be remiss were I not to note that the twin pillars of psychoanalysis, Sigmund Freud and Carl Jung, were both fascist sympathizers. In 1933—the year that Adolf Hitler and the Nazi Party ascended to power—Germany's influential *Journal of Psychotherapy* published an article by Dr. M.H. Goering, a cousin of Hermann Goering, urging psychotherapists to make "a serious scientific study of Adolf Hitler's fundamental work *Mein Kampf*, and to recognize it as a basic work." The editor of the journal openly calling for the Nazification of psychotherapy was Dr. Carl Gustav Jung.

Sigmund Freud had close ties to the Reich as well, particularly to a man named George Viereck – the illegitimate grandson of the Kaiser who had ties to *SS Reichsfuhrer* Heinrich Himmler and was perhaps the most avid supporter of Nazism in America. Viereck ran an extensive pro-Hitler propaganda operation that included having a US Senator on his payroll—Ernest Lundeen from Minnesota—whose hastily scheduled flight out of Washington following the revelation of his connection to Viereck conveniently crashed on August 31, 1940, as such flights are prone to do.

In 1926, Viereck interviewed Freud—whom he had known for many years—on the subject of anti-Semitism, and in 1930 published that interview in a collection entitled *Glimpses of the Great*.

Freud would later state that: "I can highly recommend the
Gestapo to everyone." And since wherever Nazis congregate, US
intelligence is never far away, it's not surprising that Freud had
impressive connections to the 'Old Boys' network as well.
Particularly close was William Bullit, who spent several months
working with Freud in Vienna and personally escorted the doctor
out of the country.

What then is this thing we call 'psychology'? Put in the simplest
possible terms, it is just another appendage of the national security infrastructure designed to attain social control and enforce
conformity to the fascist state. It in fact is nearly indistinguishable
from the American criminal justice/penal system. There is at least
one major difference though – the psychiatrist is allowed to serve
as prosecutor, judge and jury in seeking the involuntary confine-
ment of 'deviants' in mental institutions that are indiscernible in
form and function from America's rapidly growing prison complex.

The harsh reality is that psychology has little to do with better-
ing the human condition and alleviating suffering, and everything
to do with lending legitimacy to the corporate capitalist state and
justifying as individual failings the ever increasing levels of suffering inflicted by the state onto society. As Frederick Winslow
Taylor—the exalted father of 'scientific management,' an early
euphemism for the deskilling of labor and the reduction of the
American labor force to interchangeable, easily exploited automa-
tons—so succinctly stated many decades ago: "in the past the man
had been first; in the future the system must be first."

Not long ago, my teenage daughter asked me why it was that so
many people she has met in her life suffer from low self-esteem.
Why indeed? The answer, it turns out, is quite simple: we are all
victims of one of the big lies of American society – the one that

says that if we educate ourselves, work hard, and apply our talents, there is absolutely nothing we cannot achieve.

We are taught from birth that anyone in this great country can rise up to the highest strata of society if they so choose – that if we have the drive and ability, nothing can hold us back. George W. Bush articulated this very message from the campaign trail recently when he said: "One of the wonderful things about America is, it doesn't matter who you are or where you're from. If you work hard, dream big, the notion of owning your own business applies to everybody."

Conversely, if we should fail we have no one but ourselves to blame, for we must not be smart enough, talented enough, or educated enough – or we just didn't try hard enough. The brutal reality though is that in the real world, the sons of the rich and powerful will assume their fathers' seats in the boardrooms of America regardless of their qualifications (George, Jr. being a prime example), while the most talented of kids from America's 'inner cities' will live and die without ever seeing the world beyond the confines of their neighborhoods.

That is the reality for the majority of Americans. And yet we are encouraged, in fact *required*, to set goals for ourselves that are impossible to attain – to buy into the Big Lie. When we inevitably fail to achieve these goals, which the social structure has deliberately put out of our reach, we are required to blame only ourselves. The system has not failed you, *you* have failed because *you* are a fucking loser. You're too fucking lazy to succeed. You're too fucking stupid to succeed. So stop looking for scapegoats and accept the fact that *you* determine your own fate.

That is what the system would have you believe. And it is, in the final analysis, the psychologist's primary job to reinforce that message. That is why it is that the nation that heralds itself as the truest form of 'democracy' is home to more psychiatrists, psychologists, therapists, counselors, social workers and psychic friends than any nation in the world. Not coincidentally, that same nation is also home to the world's largest penal system. That, apparently, is the price we pay for 'freedom' in this country, a peculiar kind of freedom that does not include the right to engage in any sort of 'deviant' behavior.

Freedom of that type, it seems, could conceivably pose a threat to the powers that be, lest too many people begin to question the 'right' of the wealthy and powerful to maintain their positions at the top of the food chain at the expense of the psychologically enslaved masses whose labors serve to fatten their investment portfolios. Better that we remain, in the words of George Orwell, in a state of "controlled insanity" – for nothing could pose a greater threat to the system than a sane population fighting for survival in an insane world.

Chapter 29

Genomes and Eugenics

Anyone who interprets National Socialism merely as a political move-
ment knows almost nothing about it. It is more than religion; it is the
determination to create a new man.

Adolf Hitler

On June 26 of 2000, the successful completion of the mapping
of the human genome was triumphantly announced. The
media were nearly universal in heaping praise on this alleged scientific milestone. This was just as true for the 'progressive' press
as it was for the more mainstream media outlets. For instance, the
World Socialist Web Site—allegedly one of the most uncompro-
misingly leftist of news sources—gushed that:

"The publication of the rough draft of the completed
sequence of the human genome on June 26 was an outstand-
ing scientific achievement, the outcome of an international
collaboration spanning a decade and involving hundreds of
scientists. The researchers used the most advanced sequencing
machines and analysed the resulting data with the aid of powerful computers ...

"The elaboration of the human genome sequence is a major
step in demystifying the evolution of the human species and
the workings of the human body. Aided by technology, such

scientific discoveries puncture the clouds of superstition that surround human existence and weaken the grip of religion over the minds of men and women."

Seemingly the only critical voice among the mindless back-slappers of the US media belonged to Robert Lederman, columnist for the *Greenwich Village Gazette*. In an insightful column featured on the *Konformist* web site, Lederman noted that:

"Probably the single greatest irony in the human genome issue is the idea being marketed to the public that this scientific advance will lead to the average person enjoying a much longer and healthier life. In light of governmental resistance to preventing corporate pollution of the environment, developing renewable sources of energy, banning the use of toxic chemicals and insecticides or protecting the food supply from contamination, can we really expect that this technology will be used to extend human life generally?

"Politicians claim there is an imminent crisis facing the social security system right now. How much worse will that crisis be if tens of millions of Americans who might otherwise have died in their sixties and seventies from chronic disease live into their nineties and beyond? Be assured that those in control have no intention of allowing this to happen.

"The far likelier scenario is that for the very wealthy there will indeed be new and miraculous medical treatments to prolong and enhance life. For the vast majority however, this new technology will only be used to further limit their freedom and privacy while creating a caste system based on genetics that fundamentally changes the way society is structured."

Lederman's concerns are well founded. What the rest of the media seem to have overlooked, deliberately or out of ignorance, is that the Human Genome Project did not arise in a vacuum. Rather, it is but the latest step in a 'scientific' progression spanning at least the last 150 years. The aforementioned *World Socialist Web Site* appeared to acknowledge this in their coverage of the much-heralded event:

"In 1838 Matthias Jakob Schleiden and Theodor Schwann discovered the cell as the fundamental unit of life. In 1859 Charles Darwin published *On the Origin of Species*, which elaborated a mechanism of evolution and set a coherent framework for all the biological sciences. In 1865 the Austrian monk Gregor Mendel developed the foundations of modern genetics. T.H. Morgan in 1910 determined that genes are organised along chromosomes. In 1942 researchers established that genes are made of DNA, a chemical found in the cell nucleus. In 1953, James Watson and Francis Crick elaborated the structure of DNA. In 1973 Stanley Cohen and Herbert Brown invented genetic engineering by transplanting a gene between bacteria, and in 1990 the Human Genome Project began."

The only problem with this capsule history of the events leading up to the cracking of the genetic code is that it is woefully incomplete. So incomplete, in fact, that it thoroughly obscures the goals being pursued by those who would claim to be working for the betterment of human civilization. This is to be expected of course when the coverage is coming from the corporate mass-media, though one expects a little better from the 'alternative' press. To see just how far off the mark this historical narrative actually is, it is instructive to review a few key events that do not appear in the timeline above.

In 1869, British psychologist Francis Galton, a cousin of Charles Darwin, published the first major document of the modern eugenics movement—*Hereditary Genius*—in which he made the observation that: "The average intellectual standard of the negro is some two grades below our own." Galton proposed that a system of arranged marriages between men of distinction and women of wealth would ultimately yield a 'gifted' race.

He based this theory on the observation that the most prominent members of British society tended to also have prominent parents (no shit, Frank? Did you figure that out all by yourself?). Two years later, the exalted Charles Darwin published *Descent of Man*—his follow-up to *Origin of Species*—in which he frequently quoted from his cousin's racist screed.

Charles Darwin had not, by the way, coined the term 'survival of the fittest' in his earlier work. That concept was first proposed by Thomas Malthus as a purely economic principal, and one that was designed—not coincidentally—to justify the rise of the capitalist state. Darwin had taken that principal and transformed it into an irrefutable natural law.

As Engels put it: "The whole Darwinist teaching of the struggle for existence is simply a transference from society to living nature of … the bourgeois doctrine of competition together with Malthus' theory of population … the same theories are transferred back again from organic nature into history and it is now claimed that their validity as eternal laws of human society has been proved."

In 1875, "coolies, convicts, and prostitutes" were declared "undesirable" aliens and excluded by newly drafted laws from immigrating to the shores of America. The next year, John Harvey Kellogg became the superintendent of the Western Health Reform

Institute, changing its name to the Battle Creek Sanitarium. Nearly fifty years later, John D. Rockefeller, Jr. would spend time at the sanitarium after suffering a 'nervous breakdown.'

Under Kellogg's directorship, the sanitarium began experimenting with 'health foods,' closely paralleling the *Lebensreform* movement in Germany. *Lebensreform* sanitariums promoted a back-to-nature ideology that espoused health foods, vegetarianism, abstention from alcohol and tobacco, and homeopathy. Kellogg would remain at Battle Creek as director until 1943, a span of sixty-seven years.

In 1882, "lunatics and idiots" joined "coolies, convicts, and prostitutes" on the list of unwanted immigrants, though numerous lunatics and idiots already living here were allowed to stay and retain their positions within the US government. The following year, Galton published his next manifesto—*Human Faculty*—in which he introduced to the world the term 'eugenics.' In 1895, Dr. Alfred Ploetz—an esteemed German eugenics researcher—published *The Excellence of Our Race and the Protection of the Weak*, which not surprisingly was far more concerned with the extermination of the weak than with their protection.

Six years later, in 1901, John D. Rockefeller founded the Rockefeller Institute for Medical Research, which quickly became a funding conduit for eugenics research. Two years later, the list of undesirable immigrants became a little longer as "epileptics and insane persons" were added. The next year, The Carnegie Institution of Washington established a research center under the directorship of Harvard-educated eugenicist Charles Benedict Davenport, with additional funding from Mary Harriman – the widow of railroad magnate Edward H. Harriman.

Meanwhile, Davenport's counterpart in Germany—Dr. Ploetz—founded the German Society for Racial Hygiene and a 'scientific' journal – the *Archive for Racial and Social Biology*.

Davenport would serve as the director of genetics for the Station for Experimental Evolution at Cold Springs Harbor on Long Island, New York until 1934. Edward Harriman was, by the way, a monopolist closely tied to the Rockefellers and was the father of Averell and Roland Harriman. In 1898, he had gained control of the Union Pacific Railroad with credit arranged by William Rockefeller, who was—like Standard Oil founder John D. Rockefeller—a son of William Avery 'Devil Bill' Rockefeller.

In 1906, the city of San Francisco ordered the segregation of all Japanese, Chinese, and Korean children in a separate school, where they could be kept a safe distance from the genetically superior white children. Elsewhere in the world, Cyril Burt—a future leading light of the eugenics movement—graduated from Oxford University and traveled to Germany to complete his studies. The next year, the state of Indiana passed the world's first compulsory sterilization laws, applicable to all "confirmed criminals, idiots, rapists and imbeciles" in state institutions. Meanwhile, "imbeciles and feeble-minded persons" were added to the still-growing list of persons excluded under US immigration laws. It obviously wasn't a good year for imbeciles.

1910 proved to be a busy year for the eugenics crowd. The Harriman family financed the building of the Eugenics Record Office as a branch of London's Galton National Laboratory, with additional financial assistance coming from John D. Rockefeller; Davenport was appointed director. That same year, reputed anti-fascist Winston Churchill was appointed Home Secretary of the UK and secretly proposed the sterilization of 100,000 "mental degenerates." Cyril Burt busied himself with revising US IQ tests for use in the UK, while John Kellogg began delivering speeches on "race degeneracy."

The next year, Davenport published *Heredity in Relation to Eugenics*. In the UK, Galton died and a Eugenics Chair was established at the University of London as per his will. In 1912, the University of London hosted the First International Congress of Eugenics, presided over by Major Leonard Darwin, the son of Charles; vice presidents prominently in attendance included Winston Churchill, Dr. Alfred Ploetz, Harvard president Charles W. Eliot, and Alexander Graham Bell.

Meanwhile, eminent psychologist Henry Goddard was having a busy year: he published *The Kallikak Family: A Study in the Heredity of Feeble Mindedness*, and also administered IQ tests to immigrants at Ellis Island and found that 83% of Jews, 80% of Hungarians, 79% of Italians, and 87% of the Russians wanting to enter the country were feeble minded. There's no telling how many of them were coolies or imbeciles.

Professor Goddard also believed that criminals could be identified by certain physical characteristics, and that the solution was "to sterilize them, allow them to perform only lowly jobs, confine them to ghettos, discourage them from marrying outside their race, and create a pure, American, superior intelligence to control them." His ideas would later have a profound influence on Dr. David Ewen Cameron.

In 1913, Rockefeller established the Rockefeller Foundation, which would serve as yet another source of funding for the eugenics movement. By this time, twelve US states had compulsory sterilization laws on the books. The next year, Battle Creek, Michigan hosted the First National Congress on Race Betterment—sponsored by John Harvey Kellogg—which proposed that 5.76 million Americans be sterilized.

Eugenics was by then being taught at Universities around the country, including Harvard, Columbia, Cornell, Brown, Wisconsin, Northwestern, and Clark. In 1915, Michigan hosted the Second National Conference on Race Betterment, again sponsored by John Harvey Kellogg. The next year, Stanford University professor of psychology Lewis M. Terman published the Stanford-Binet IQ tests, while declaring that: "If we would preserve our state for a class of people worthy to possess it, we would prevent, as far as possible, the propagation of mental degenerates."

In 1920, Alfred Hoche and Karl Binding published *The Release of the Destruction of Life Devoid of Value*, advocating "euthanasia" for mentally defective and mentally ill persons. By this time, twenty-four other states had joined Indiana in passing compulsory sterilization laws. In 1921, New York hosted the Second International Congress of Eugenics, sponsored by a committee that included Herbert Hoover and the presidents of Clark University, Smith College and the Carnegie Institution.

Also that year, president Warren G. Harding approved the Immigration Restriction Act, establishing a quota system, and Margaret Sanger published an article entitled "The Eugenic Value of Birth Control Propaganda" in the journal *Birth Control Review*. Sanger was concerned that "the fertility of the feeble-minded, the mentally defective, the poverty-stricken classes, should not be held up for emulation to the mentally and physically fit though less fertile parents of the educated and well-to-do classes. On the contrary, the most urgent problem today is how to limit and discourage the over fertility of the mentally and physically defective."

The next year, H.H. Laughlin published the "Model Eugenical Sterilization Law," declaring all of the following categories of persons as being subject to mandatory sterilization: feeble-minded, insane, criminalistic, epileptic, inebriate, diseased, blind and seriously vision impaired, deformed and crippled, and dependent (orphans, homeless persons, tramps, and paupers). This law would serve as the blueprint for several US state sterilization laws as well as for Nazi Germany's infamous 1933 eugenics law. That same year, the American Eugenics Society was founded on the proposition that the wealth and social position of the upper classes was justified by their superior genetic endowment.

In 1923, Carl Brigham—a key figure in the development of IQ tests and the driving force behind the SAT—published *The Study of American Intelligence*, declaring that: "our figures, then, would rather tend to disprove the popular belief that the Jew is intelligent," and "The decline of American intelligence will be more rapid than the decline of the intelligence of European national groups owing to the presence here of the Negro." In Germany, Adolf Hitler allegedly dictated—from a jail cell—the first draft of the virulently racist and anti-Semitic *Mein Kampf*, which singled out Henry Ford for praise.

The following year, the Johnson-Reed act (*aka* the Immigration Act of 1924) eliminated Asian immigration and set stringent quotas on Southern and Eastern European immigration. In 1925, US Supreme Court Justice Oliver Wendell Holmes—writing the majority opinion in Buck *v.* Bell—stated: "It is better for all the world, if instead of waiting to execute degenerate offspring for crime or to let them starve for their imbecility, society can prevent those who are manifestly unfit from continuing their kind," language that closely mirrored that of Hitler's *Mein Kampf*. In the UK that same year, Cyril Burt—who specialized in twin studies (first suggested by Galton) and who would later become one of the founding fathers of Mensa—published *The Young Delinquent*.

In 1928, Battle Creek, Michigan hosted the Third National Conference on Race Betterment, once again sponsored by John Harvey Kellogg. In 1930, the director of the Department of Heredity at the Kaiser Wilhelm Institute for Genealogy and Demography—Dr. Ernst Rudin—visited the United States, where he was warmly received. Rudin walked away with a large grant from the Rockefeller Foundation to finance his research, which would occupy an entire floor at the Kaiser Wilhelm Institute.

Elsewhere, W.K. Kellogg established the W.K. Kellogg Foundation to provide funding for efforts at "social improvement."

By 1931, twenty-seven US states had sterilization laws, and John Kellogg had opened the Miami-Battle Creek Sanitarium in Miami Springs, Florida with himself appointed as medical director. That year also saw an indeterminate number of Puerto Ricans deliberately infected with cancer by the Rockefeller Institute, killing thirteen. Pathologist Cornelius Rhoades, who ran the study, was later placed in charge of two chemical warfare projects and granted a seat on the Atomic Energy Commission.

1932 saw New York's American Museum of Natural History host the Third International Congress of Eugenics, at which the sterilization of fourteen million Americans was called for. The gathering was dedicated to Mary Harriman. The Hamburg-Amerika Shipping Line—one of the subsidiaries of Brown Brothers/Harriman seized in 1942 by the US Alien Property Custodian—provided transportation to America for a sizable number of Nazis to attend the conference. Included among them was Dr. Rudin, who was unanimously elected president of the International Federation of Eugenics Societies.

The following year, Hitler enacted the Law for the Prevention of Hereditary Diseases in Posterity, drafted by Dr. Rudin and patterned directly after H.H. Laughlin's 1922 model. In 1935, Nazi Germany instituted the Law for the Protection of the Genetic Health of the German People, which mandated medical examinations prior to marriage. Also begun that year was a selective human breeding program known as *Lebensborn*—under the direction of Hitler's rabidly fascist *SS* Chief, Heinrich Himmler—which all *SS* men were obligated to join. By 1946, some 11,000 of 'Hitler's Children' were created on breeding farms. In nearby England, Cyril Burt published *The Subnormal Mind*.

On the distant shores of America, Dr. Alexis Carrel—a Nobel laureate and a close associate of Charles Lindbergh (the two had worked together on a 'research project' at the Rockefeller Institute laboratory in 1934)—published *Man, the Unknown*, declaring: "There remains the unsolved problem of the immense number of defectives and criminals. They are an enormous burden for the part of the population that has remained normal ... In Germany, the government has taken energetic measures against the multiplication of inferior types, the insane and criminals ... Perhaps prisons should be abolished. They could be replaced by smaller and less expensive institutions. The conditioning of petty criminals with the whip, or some more scientific procedure, followed by a short stay in hospital, would probably suffice to insure order. Those who have [committed more serious crimes] should be humanely and economically disposed of in small euthanasia institutions supplied with proper gasses. A similar treatment could be advantageously applied to the insane, guilty of criminal acts. Modern society should not hesitate to organize itself with reference to the normal individual."

In 1937, Cyril Burt published yet another eugenically minded tome, which he titled *The Backward Child*. This year was also notable for the establishment of the Pioneer Fund, yet another thinly veiled cover for the funding of eugenics research. As late as 1989, the organization would still state in its (revised) charter that its express purpose was to finance "study into the problems of human race betterment."

With the outbreak of World War II, the genocidal agenda behind the rapidly proliferating eugenics foundations was revealed to the world, and the movement had to temporarily retreat to the fetid swamps and sewers from which it had emerged. It wasn't dead, however, but was merely "forced to reinvent itself under various fronts," as columnist Robert Lederman has noted.

After the war, psychiatrist Edwin Katzen-ellenbogen—a former member of the faculty at Harvard—was convicted of war crimes that he had committed as a 'doctor' at Buchenwald concentration camp; during his trial in Dachau, he proudly testified that he had drafted the sterilization law for the governor of New Jersey.

Around 1948, Mensa was formed – the first international organization for the intellectually 'gifted.' Its first president was preeminent eugenicist Cyril Burt, who had been named the president of the British Psychological Society in 1942 and had become the first psychologist to be knighted in 1946. Another founding father was Victor Serebriakoff, a White Russian émigré recruited by British and American intelligence services who was credited with greatly expanding membership in the organization, instituting the IQ test as a prerequisite of membership, and establishing American Mensa. Yet another founder, and the man who claimed to have come up with the idea for Mensa, was Dr. Lance Ware, a biochemist who had worked during World War II at Porton Down – Britain's ultra-secret biological and chemical warfare facility.

1948 was also the year that Franz Kallman, who had been an associate of Ernst Rudin, founded a new eugenics institute dubbed the American Society of Human Genetics. Around that same time, Dr. Otmar von Verschuer, who had served as the mentor of the notorious Josef Mengele, founded the Institute of Human Genetics in Munster. The next year, the Atomic Energy Commission and the Quaker Oats company fed a group of 'retarded' boys in Massachusetts radioactive cereal; John Kellogg would have been proud.

In 1950, Cyril Burt published the results of some of his twin studies, purportedly showing data that supported his eugenics views. His studies claimed to prove that poverty was due to the intellectual inferiority of the working class. In 1952, John Foster Dulles established the Population Council in conjunction with

John D. Rockefeller III. Tens of millions of dollars of Rockefeller grant money were pumped in as the American Eugenics Society moved its headquarters into the offices of—and assumed the name of—the newly created Population Council.

In 1960, Reginald Gates, a member of the American Eugenics Society, began publishing Mankind Quarterly, a fountain of thinly veiled racist propaganda. On the Advisory Council of the periodical sat none other than Charles Galton Darwin – a grandson of Charles who had written the eugenically minded tome *The Next Million Years* in 1952. Another advisor, as well as a member of the Eugenics Society, was Dr. von Verschuer.

By 1967, Nobel prize winner William Shockley was rewriting history with his conclusion that: "The lesson to be drawn from Nazi history is the value of free speech, not that eugenics is intolerable." Also that year, three psychosurgeons—Vernon H. Marks, Frank R. Ervin, and William H. Sweet—published a letter in the *Journal of the American Medical Association* in which they theorized that brain disease was responsible for rising levels of urban violence and the uprisings that were rocking America's cities.

The National Institute of Mental Health promptly awarded the trio $500,000 to investigate the use of psychosurgery on violence-prone individuals. The next year, James Dewey Watson—co-discoverer of the molecular structure of DNA—began serving as the director of the Cold Springs Harbor Laboratory of Quantitative Biology. Twenty years later, he would lend his expertise to the Human Genome Project.

1972 found Shockley delivering an address before the American Psychological Association in which he called for a program in which welfare recipients would be paid $1,000 for each IQ point below 100 if they would submit to voluntary sterilization. In 1976, Cyril Burt's research was denounced and declared to be fraudulent. London's *Sunday Times* reported that his two 'field investigators' and 'co-authors' were complete fabrications; Burt himself had authored articles for fifteen years under assumed names praising his own work and attacking his critics. He was posthumously declared guilty of fraud by the British Psychological Society.

In 1978, another eugenically minded foundation—the Manhattan Institute—was founded by future CIA Director William Casey, who sixteen years prior had co-founded another New York City 'think tank' with Prescott Bush. The primary corporate sponsor was the Rockefeller-controlled Chase Manhattan Bank; others included Citicorp, Time Warner, Proctor & Gamble, Bristol-Meyers, Squibb, CIGNA and Lilly.

The next year, the Repository for Germinal Choice was set up in Escondido, California to make available the sperm of Nobel prize winners and other 'intelligent' people for selective breeding. Ads were run in Mensa publications and Shockley became one of the first donors. 1982 saw the first of the new breed of Hitler's Children spawned from sperm obtained from the Repository for Germinal Choice.

In 1989, George Bush became the 41st President of the United States. The very next year, the Human Genome Project was launched by James Watson at Cold Springs Harbor Laboratory on Long Island, New York. In 1993, a new manifesto for the modern-day eugenics crowd was published: *The Bell Curve*. The book was sponsored by the Pioneer Fund, a major supporter and source of funding for the Manhattan Institute; the Institute itself held a luncheon to honor the book and its authors.

In November of 2000, Watson delivered a speech at the University of California at Berkeley that outraged many of those in attendance. Among other undocumented claims, Watson suggested that there exist biochemical links between skin color and

sexual activity. And so it goes as the eugenics movement continues
to flourish under cover of scientific jargon.

That the Human Genome Project (HGP) is in fact yet another
front for the eugenics movement can be easily discerned from a
visit to the program's web site. There you will find that the haunt-
ingly familiar goals of the project include "earlier detection of
genetic predisposition to disease" and "reduc(ing) the likelihood
of heritable mutations." In other words, one goal is the systematic
elimination of all the 'bad' genes that have slipped into the
national pool.

Another goal of the project is the creation of "pharmacoge-
nomics 'custom drugs.'" Translated into English, this means drugs
that are specifically tailored to differentially affect various genetic
(racial) types; drugs, that is, that could easily be wielded as ethnically specific biowarfare agents. The development of such
weapons has been an explicit goal of the US military for at least a
quarter-century. In 1975, an American military manual candidly
noted that:

"It is theoretically possible to develop so-called 'ethnic chemical
weapons,' which would be designed to exploit naturally occurring
differences in vulnerability among specific population groups.
Thus, such a weapon would be capable of incapacitating or killing
a selected enemy population to a significantly greater extent than
the population of friendly forces."

Strangely enough, in the years since those words were written "at
least 30 previously unknown disease agents have been identified,"
according to our very own Central Intelligence Agency. Many of
these—including AIDS, Ebola, and the Four Corners Virus—without
question show a distinct preference for certain ethnic groups that
have long been targets of depopulation campaigns.

Interestingly, the HGP touts as another of its benefits the potential for "protection from biological and chemical warfare." Of
course, as the US government itself has acknowledged on numer-

ous occasions, research into *protection* from biowarfare requires concomitant research into the *conductance* of biowarfare; the two are, in practice, inseparable.

Meanwhile, Mensa—which claims disingenuously to hold no opinions and promote no agenda—continues by all appearances to function as an intelligence front, including serving at times as a mouthpiece for the eugenics movement. One of the organization's 'Special Interest Groups' is titled, simply enough, *Eugenics*, and the pages of various Mensa publications are known to this day to host 'intellectual' discussions of the benefits of eugenics policies.

From their beginnings the movements overlapped. Scientific management, intelligence testing, applied psychology, mental hygiene, and eugenics became fashionable together and were often espoused by the same people ... Throughout the West, the erosion of older structures of class and authority, and the claims and challenges of new classes and ethnic groups, stimulated the work of the phrenologists, the testers of intelligence, the eugenicists, and the analysts of deviance—Lombroso, Binet, Madison Grant, and, in the first half of the twentieth century, Cyril Burt, Edward L. Thorndike, H.M. Goddard, Lewis M. Terman, and Sheldon and Eleanor Glueck; but it was in America—necessarily in America, that most democratic, 'classless,' and ethnically pluralistic society—where they became most influential.

Peter Schrag *Mind Control*, Pantheon, 1978

Chapter 30

Genocide, by Natural Causes

Many readers are doubtless unaware of the fact that several researchers have put forth compelling cases arguing that the AIDS 'virus' was developed specifically as a biowarfare agent. This is primarily due to the fact that whenever evidence in support of this theory has been uncovered, it has been consistently ignored by the media, even when coming from respected, knowledgeable sources in the medical and scientific communities.

It is not my intent to join in that debate here. The issue of concern here is whether—regardless of the *origins* of the virus—AIDS is being *utilized* as a biowarfare agent. In other words, even if AIDS *is* a naturally occurring virus, has it been used as—or at the very least allowed to function as—a biowarfare agent? This is a much easier question to answer – and the answer is that it clearly has.

Painfully obvious is the fact that in the US, the victims of AIDS have overwhelmingly come from marginalized groups that have not historically found favor with the ruling elite: Blacks, gays, and intravenous drug users. It may surprise some—who still view

AIDS as being a gay disease—to see Blacks listed first in that grouping.

The fact is that while the disease initially seemed to primarily target the gay population, it is in truth first and foremost a killer of people of color. It has been recently reported by the *Los Angeles Times* that the "CDC estimates that about 40,000 new [AIDS] infections occur in the United States each year, with about half of those among African Americans and about 15% among Latinos." In other words, fully two-thirds of new AIDS victims are persons of color.

Also reported in the *Times* article was that "HIV infection rates are alarmingly high among African Americans in some northeastern and southern US cities." The *Irish Times* has added that: "AIDS is now the single biggest cause of death among African-American men aged between 25 and 40, who are now 10 times more likely to die of the disease than whites." While this certainly presents a disturbing picture, domestic patterns of infection are not of great concern for the purposes of this discussion.

What is of concern is the international impact of the AIDS virus. On a global level, infection patterns are following a parallel course to that which is occurring domestically. Blacks are far and away the primary victims of the virus, followed by other non-white races. In fact, as the *Times* noted, the entire continent of Africa appears to be on the verge of a massive depopulation.

"Nearly three-quarters of the 34 million people living with AIDS reside in sub-Saharan Africa, and deaths are increasing at a rate that scientists would have found incomprehensible only a few years ago. Since the beginning of the AIDS epidemic, 11.5 million people have died of the disease in sub-Saharan Africa. About 5,500 now die of AIDS every day, but researchers predict that about 13,000 will die daily by 2010."

Dr. Roy M. Anderson of Oxford University, speaking at the 13th International AIDS Conference, called this "undoubtedly the most serious infectious disease threat in recorded human history." Another speaker, Karen Stanecki of the US Census Bureau, projected that "by 2010, life expectancy will be 29 in Botswana, 30 in Swaziland, 33 in Namibia and Zimbabwe, and 36 in South Africa, Malawi and Rwanda. Without AIDS, it would have been around 70 in many of those countries."

The UN has reported that "the disease is expected to wipe out half the teen-agers in some African nations, devastating economies and societies." Peter Piot, who heads the UN Joint Program on HIV/AIDS, told a press conference that: "There is a whole generation which is being taken out ... The probability that you die from AIDS when you are 15 today is over 50% in these countries."

And what has been the response of the world community to this unprecedented humanitarian crisis? According to a report issued by the United Nations Children's Fund—otherwise known as UNICEF—it has been a collective shrug. The report, described by the *L.A. Times* as "scorching," bluntly denounces the world's response—or rather lack thereof—to the suffering in Africa.

"The HIV infection rates among young people are a searing indictment, documenting failures of vision, commitment and action of almost unbelievable proportions ... They tell a story of leadership unworthy of the name and the virtual abandonment of sub-Saharan Africa at a time of dire need."

But what if the lack of response noted by UNICEF is not due to simple *inaction,* but is due rather to a specific plan of action that calls for *deliberate non-action?* What if the inaction is itself the plan of action? A thoughtful reading of a recent CIA report—as well as some comments coming out of the White House—reveals that this may well be the case.

It seems that it is not true that the United States has failed to formulate a response to the AIDS crisis – it's just that Washington has failed to formulate a response to AIDS as a *health issue*. That's because the wise men who rule America recognize that AIDS should not be viewed as a global health crisis; it should be viewed as a *national security threat*.

This was stated rather explicitly by White House spokesman Jim Kennedy in April of 2000, when he noted that AIDS, "more than an ongoing health threat, also has the potential to destabilize governments such as African and Asian nations, which make it an international security issue."

This notion was seconded in May by Clinton spokesman Joe Lockhart, who referred to the number of AIDS deaths in Africa as "staggering" and "destabilizing," adding that "they have an impact on us. We have an interest in Africa, as far as our own national security, and we need to look at this problem—as the NSC has done, very much so this year, but going back over the last couple of years—as a national security issue."

The CIA report—the declassified version of which was released in early 2000—elaborates considerably on the statements made by the White House mouthpieces: the overt US response to the AIDS crisis will come not in the form of medical assistance, but in the form of 'humanitarian' military aid.

The report begins by proclaiming itself to be "an important initiative on the part of the Intelligence Community to consider the national security dimensions of a nontraditional threat." This nontraditional threat is, of course, the rising global death toll due to not just AIDS, but to a host of "new and reemerging diseases [that will] complicate US and global security over the next 20 years."

In addition to "at least 30 previously unknown disease agents [that] have been identified since 1973, including HIV, Ebola,

hepatitis C, and Nipah virus, for which no cures are available,"
another "twenty well-known diseases—including tuberculosis
(TB), malaria, and cholera—have reemerged or spread
geographically since 1973, often in more virulent and drug-
resistant forms."

The report is notably lacking in any explanation for this
unprecedented explosion of emerging and reemerging diseases in
the last quarter-century. There is clearly no comparable period in
recorded human history. Neither has there ever been a virus that
discriminated by ethnicity. The report offers no comments on this
phenomenon either.

Readers who have been paying close attention may have
noticed that all fifty of these new disease threats have emerged
since 1973, which—as the last chapter noted—was the very same
year that "Stanley Cohen and Herbert Brown invented genetic
engineering by transplanting a gene between bacteria." I'm sure
there's no connection, however, as the CIA report certainly doesn't
note any.

What is noted is that some parts of the world are decidedly
more affected by the AIDS crisis than are others, specifically
those areas that have traditionally been the target of covert
destabilization efforts: "Developing and former communist
countries will continue to experience the greatest impact from
infectious diseases."

The most heavily impacted area will be, of course, sub-Saharan
Africa, which now accounts for "nearly half of infectious disease
deaths globally." It is not alone, however. "Asia and the Pacific ...
is likely to witness a dramatic increase in infectious disease deaths,
largely driven by the spread of HIV/AIDS in South and Southeast
Asia ... By 2010, the region could surpass Africa in the number of
HIV infections."

Next on the CIA's list of the most seriously impacted areas is our long-time nemesis, "the former Soviet Union (FSU) and, to a lesser extent, Eastern Europe [which] also are likely to see a substantial increase in infectious disease incidence and deaths." While the people of this area are not as susceptible to the AIDS virus, "TB has reached epidemic proportions throughout the FSU."

The situation is not likely to improve in these nations anytime soon. In fact, the report predicts that "some of the hardest hit countries in Sub-Saharan Africa—and possibly later in South and Southeast Asia—will face a demographic upheaval as HIV/AIDS and associated diseases reduce human life expectancy by as much as 30 years and kill as many as a quarter of their populations over a decade or less."

This massive loss of human life will have profound effects on the political, economic, and social systems of the afflicted nations. As the authors note: "The persistent infectious disease burden is likely to aggravate and, in some cases, may even provoke economic decay, social fragmentation, and political destabilization in the hardest hit countries in the developing and former communist worlds."

It is precisely at this point—when a massive depopulation has occurred, resulting in the collapse of the prevailing socio-economic order—that US interests become 'threatened,' thereby necessitating American involvement. This will become increasingly likely as the destabilizing effects of the rising death tolls "challenge democratic development and transitions and possibly contribute to humanitarian emergencies and military conflicts to which the United States may need to respond."

It should be noted here that the CIA actually has no interest whatsoever in "democratic development and transitions." The agency's primary function for 53 years now has been not the promotion of democracy, but the universal extension of Western capitalism to every corner of the globe. And it is in precisely those areas of the world now facing a "nontraditional threat" that the greatest resistance to the imposition of Western capitalist rule has long found a home.

How convenient then for the Western powers that those areas that have long served as targets of a wide variety of destabilization efforts and techniques are now faced with the prospect of being destabilized by a 'naturally' occurring viral agent. Even more convenient is that the destabilization will occur in such a way that it will allow the US to step in and restore order—or rather replace it with a US-approved form of order—under the pretext of responding to a health crisis.

The basic game-plan seems to go something like this: first, allow the disease to fester unattended, permeating certain areas of the world. Next—while feigning concern and giving lip-service to doing something about the ensuing crisis—continue to do as little as possible while a massive depopulation takes place, shattering the social order. Then, under the pretense of responding to a humanitarian emergency, send in the 'peacekeeping' troops to militarily occupy the besieged country.

This final phase of the plan will be aided considerably by the fact that an enormous portion of the fighting-age men and women in the targeted countries will have been exterminated. In fact, the highest rates of HIV/AIDS infections in the sub-Saharan countries is in, conveniently enough, the military services.

"HIV/AIDS prevalence in selected militaries, mostly in sub-Saharan Africa ... is considerably higher than their civilian populations ... given that a large number of officers and other key personnel are dying or becoming disabled, combat readiness and capability of such military forces is bound to deteriorate."

Incredibly enough, the report finds that infection rates among military personnel in countries such as Angola and the

Democratic Republic of Congo—both longtime targets of CIA covert operations—are an astonishing 40-60%, with these numbers continuing to grow in most militaries surveyed by the report's authors.

How, you may wonder, does the CIA account for this rather remarkable anomaly of the global AIDS crisis? By attributing, rather disingenuously, the appallingly high rates of infection to "risky lifestyles and deployment away from home." Nice explanation, except that it makes no intuitive sense whatsoever.

First of all, there is absolutely no evidence that these men and women do in fact lead riskier lifestyles. More importantly, the notion that deployment away from home leads to higher rates of infection defies all logic. Home, it will be remembered, is where the world's highest infection rates are occurring. Deployment away from home—*anywhere* away from home—would therefore expose the servicemen to substantially *less* risk of infection.

How then this is supposed to explain away the unfathomably high infection rates being observed is anyone's guess. But the point here is that—in addition to reducing the social and economic systems to a shambles—AIDS is having an even more profound impact on the military sector of select countries.

It should go without saying that this phenomenon will greatly facilitate the military occupation of these nations. Minimal resistance will be met as the 'peacekeepers' roll into town to suck the remaining life—as well as, naturally, the wealth—out of these long-suffering areas of the world. As the CIA tacitly acknowledges:

"Mounting infectious disease-caused deaths among the military officer corps in military-dominated and democratizing polities also may contribute to the deprivation, insecurity, and political machinations that incline some to launch coups and counter-coups aimed, more often than not, at plundering state coffers."

And that, you can be sure, is a topic on which the CIA can speak with some authority.

Afterword: Understanding the F-Word – A Brief Return

The followers of Marxian socialism in Germany, split into several parties, would if united constitute the greatest force in the nation, and socialism and labor were almost synonymous in Germany. Hitler knew this. He capitalized on it. He stole the word.
George Seldes, Facts and Fascism, 1943

Many readers will no doubt have difficulty digesting the assertions made in this book. Many will argue that fascism is in fact a socialist system, not a capitalist system. And that is, of course, what we are encouraged to believe. All the evil brought forth upon this world in the last century has been the work of the dreaded communists.

I have in fact had a number of educated and seemingly rational people try to explain to me over the years how Hitler and Stalin represent two prime examples of the excesses of communism/socialism. The most obvious reason for this rather widespread misconception is that fascist movements have always cloaked themselves in the garb of socialism.

The truth though is that adopting a name is not the same thing as adopting an ideology. It's all well and good to *call* your movement the National Socialist Worker's Party, but that doesn't make it a socialist movement any more than naming your party the Reform Party makes you a reformer.

By the same token, it's all well and good for Benito Mussolini to have posed as a socialist writer for a number of years to establish his leftist credentials, but that didn't make him a socialist any more than it made Ronald Reagan a 'Democrat' to pose as one while he busied himself with ridding Hollywood of suspected 'communists.' What it did make him was a poseur, an agent provocateur[69] (Mussolini that is, though Reagan qualifies as well).

The problem with mounting an overtly fascist movement is that it will not likely garner much popular support. A movement based on an inherently anti-democratic ideology can only garner popular support by posing as a populist movement, a fact that is well understood by the Pat Buchanans of the world.

Once in office, however, the trappings of socialist populism are quickly shed, as was the case in Italy and Germany where the first target of the incoming regimes was labor (not, as the right-wingers would have you believe, gun owners). The outlawing of strikes and the destruction of labor unions was the order of the day, as was the mass arrests of leftists – who were the first victims of Nazi concentration camps.[70]

Another factor which clouds the true nature of fascism is the enduring myth, perpetuated now for six decades, of a Nazi/Red alliance during World War II. In reality, there never was such an alliance. There *was* a non-aggression pact, offered by the Nazis

---

[69] See *Sawdust Caesar: The Untold History of Mussolini and Fascism*, by George Seldes (Harper & Brothers, 1935), for what is still the best biography to date of Benito Mussolini.

[70] *Himmler's Black Order 1923-45*. The first concentration camps began to dot the German landscape in 1933, the year Hitler took power. Like many other aspects of the Reich, concentration camps were a Western innovation, originated by Great Britain.

and accepted by the Soviets shortly before the German Army
plowed through Poland.

In retrospect though, it is pretty obvious that this was a ruse by
the Nazis to hold the Soviets at bay and lull them into a false sense
of complacency as the Reich prepared a massive assault on the
Soviet frontier, and it is almost certain that the Soviets were aware
of this even as they signed the bogus offer from the Nazis.

It appears to have been something of a no-win situation for the
Soviets. Had they refused to sign, they would have been cast as the
villains for refusing the 'peace' offer from the Germans. And having signed it, of course, they were then cast as collaborators with
the Nazis.

So pervasive has been the historical pattern of draping socialist
rhetoric over a fascist agenda that it has become the way that we
are taught to view the world, indeed the very way that we are
taught to *think*. To the Western way of thinking, there are only
two possible sociopolitical systems: democracy or socialism/com-
munism.

Unfortunately, this skewed world dynamic ignores the fact that
democracy and socialism are not mutually exclusive categories.
One of them (democracy) is in fact a political system, while the
other (socialism) is an economic system. It is the juxtaposition of
the two systems—political and economic—that determines the
form of government adopted by any nation at any given time.

At one end of the political continuum lies democracy – rule of,
by and for the people. At the other end lies authoritarianism – rule
by the elite few at the expense of, and by the oppression of, the
people. Likewise, capitalism—characterized by the private ownership of the means of production—lies at one end of the economic
continuum, and at the other extreme lies socialism – the collective
ownership of that same means of production.

In practice, there are varying shades of gray along the political and economic continuums, with most economies being a mix of capitalist and socialist elements and most political systems falling somewhere between autocratic rule and true democracy. In the simplest possible terms though, there are four possible combinations of elements that comprise the basic sociopolitical systems of the world. This is best represented in a table:

	Democracy	Authoritarianism
Capitalism		
Socialism		

This is of course a gross oversimplification, for reasons already stated. It is not nearly as oversimplified though as the view of the world that we as Americans are conditioned from birth to accept as the gospel truth. From the Western point of view, the world looks something like this:

	Democracy	Authoritarianism
Capitalism	The Free World	*does not exist*
Socialism	*does not exist*	Godless Communism

In other words, we do not acknowledge that any form of socialism exists other than the brutally oppressive authoritarian socialism that we commonly refer to as 'Communism.' By the same token, we equate capitalism with democracy, refusing to acknowledge that democracy can exist independently of capitalism, or that capitalism can exist in any other form than democratic capitalism.

And where are we to place fascism in such a belief system? Since there are only two options available, and since fascism clearly does not fit into our square, then it must belong in the other one, with the communists. In truth though, the table should look more like this:

	Democracy	Authoritarianism
Capitalism	democratic capitalism	fascism
Socialism	democratic socialism	'communism'

Here we see that authoritarian capitalism not only exists, but it has a name; its name is, of course, fascism. The vast majority of Americans will readily agree that both fascism and what we call 'Communism' are undesirable systems. But the point here is that—contrary to popular opinion—they are bad systems not because they are both socialist systems, but because they are both *authoritarian, anti-democratic* systems.

In other words, it is not socialism that we should fear and loathe, it is authoritarianism – whether manifest as a capitalist or as a socialist system. The question we should be asking is not: what is the superior system – democracy or communism? The real question is: what is the superior system – *democratic* capitalism or *democratic* socialism?

This is the question that we in America would never ask. It is not that we would never *dare* to ask such a question, it's that we would never *think* to ask such a question. It is not necessary to physically oppress those who would ask such questions when psychological and educational oppression have all but eliminated the ability to formulate them. Nary a voice can be heard on the political landscape that questions the underlying legitimacy of capitalism.

The very concept of 'democratic capitalism' sounds redundant to us. Are they not one and the same? And how can we seriously compare our very real (or so we think) conception of democracy with something like "democratic socialism," which is clearly a contradiction in terms that doesn't even exist?

But if we *did* ask the question, what would the answer be? It has been argued here that the capitalist system is inherently fascistic. This really shouldn't surprise us. In a system where everything has a price tag—and this is seen as a good thing—why should we be outraged when the government shows itself to be for sale to the highest bidder? [71]

And why should we expect that the highest bidder would be anyone other than the multinational corporate behemoths? How could we expect not to be ruled by an elite few when it is precisely that elite few who are in the best position to buy and maintain the power?

The capitalist system can, of course, be modified to approximate the appearance of democracy, as has been the case throughout much of America's history. Income can be redistributed to some extent, for instance, and anti-trust legislation can be enforced, the judicial system can enforce human and civil rights protections, and labor unions can be legally protected.

But the tendency to regress (or progress, in the eyes of some) into overt fascism is strong and difficult to keep in check. Concentration of wealth is inevitable, and with it concentration of political power, the two being virtually synonymous in the capitalist state. There is, in other words, a built-in contradiction between democracy and capitalism.

---

[71] It should probably be noted here that the 'truth' is also, like every other commodity in the 'free market,' for sale to the highest bidder. That is why much of the material in this book is probably unfamiliar to the reader.

And what of this notion of democratic socialism? Has this not proven itself to be a utopian ideal that cannot work in the real world? Has it not failed everywhere it has been attempted? Many leftists believe this to be the case and have abandoned the cause.

Where then are we to look for this elusive thing we call democracy? Some, including many former leftists, are looking for answers from the so-called 'Anarchist' movement. Many in the movement are young and angry, and rightfully so. But their anger has been, as is so frequently the case, co-opted and misdirected.

For what is 'anarchy' but the complete lack of government? And having reduced society to the purest form of social Darwinism, who would rule if not corporate America? Is it not, in the final analysis, the ultimate goal of the corporate state to do away with borders and governments and reduce the world to one global marketplace? The militia groups and other right-wing organizations recognize this fact, though their outrage and resistance has been co-opted as well.

These groups tend to promote an aggressively authoritarian agenda as a way to correct the problems affiliated with the current aggressively authoritarian system. The only real difference between the agenda promoted by the militia groups and the agenda promoted by the US government is that the former tend to prefer a system of national fascism, while the latter tends to prefer a system of global fascism.

The truth is that both of these 'protest groups' (Anarchists and 'Patriots'), while appearing to be foes of the 'establishment,' are co-opted movements which have been misdirected into supporting the very system that they believe themselves to be opposing. That is, of course, the pattern that has been followed throughout this century.

In fact, those who have been deceived into endorsing the agenda of the right-wing militia movement would be well-served by studying the rise of the Third Reich in Germany. Particular attention should be paid to the night of June 30, 1934, little more than a year after Hitler had consolidated power. Known as 'The Night of the Long Knives,' that was the day that the Nazi party launched a purge of the *SA*, sometimes known as the 'Brownshirts.'

These loosely organized groups were the closest thing the Nazi party had to a populist wing. They had been the foot soldiers in the initial rise of the party. With the party firmly ensconced in power though, they had outlived their usefulness. The time had come to shed the populist baggage, and so the *SA* leadership was eliminated, their followers left in disarray. With the demise of the *SA*, Heinrich Himmler's *SS*, culled from the elite of German society, was given virtually unlimited power. [72]

Of course, most Anarchists would heatedly dispute that their movement is co-opted. For they are not just anti-government, but anti-corporation as well, in addition to supporting human and civil rights, environmental causes, and various other noble pursuits. And the vast majority of individuals within the movement are undoubtedly motivated by a sincere concern for their fellow man.

None of that, however, changes the fact that the movement is indeed co-opted, just as surely as the hippie movement and the acid culture of the 1960's was co-opted from very early on. Those movements, naturally enough, didn't feel that they were co-opted

[72] *Unholy Alliance* and *Himmler's Black Order*

either. They too felt themselves to be an anti-establishment force, taking credit for—among other things—ending the war in Vietnam.

The truth though is that the goals of the sixties activists, while noble ones, were subverted in a variety of ways, most notably by the introduction of LSD and other drugs into the movements, and by the infiltration of fraudulent leaders, sometimes following the assassination or imprisonment of the true revolutionary leaders of the era.[73]

The truth is also that most of the goals of the activists were never achieved, due largely to the co-opting of the movements. The war in Vietnam, for instance, was not brought to an end by the anti-war movement. The war in fact raged on for longer than any overt war in the history of the United States, through three presidential administrations.[74]

President Nixon, despite campaign promises to end the conflict, continued to escalate the war through his entire first term in the White House, just as Johnson before him had continued America's involvement throughout his tenure. Even after the anti-war protests reached something of a crescendo with the shooting deaths of four Kent State students at the hands of the Ohio National Guard, the war continued for another three years.

If the anti-war movement was responsible for ending the war, it certainly took its time in doing so. So long, in fact, that five

---

[73] The honest voices of leadership in the sixties were almost exclusively in the black community - men such as Malcolm X, Fred Hampton, and Dr. Martin Luther King, Jr.. These men met with quite different fates than did the icons of white America.

[74] And that was just the overt phase of the war. Covert operations had begun long before Kennedy took office, and continued long after Nixon stepped down (see William Blum's *Killing Hope* and Douglas Valentine's *The Phoenix Program*, Morrow, 1990).

million or more Southeast Asians lost their lives as a direct result of US actions in the area. The sad reality is that once the acid gurus gained control of the movement, it never had a chance.

False prophets like Timothy Leary, Richard "Baba Ram Dass" Alpert, Ken Kesey and Aldous Huxley, all of whom had extensive connections to a web of intelligence operatives,[75] co-opted the movement by instructing the faithful to "turn on, tune in, and drop out," precisely the wrong message to deliver.

As soon as the anti-war movement adopted the ideology of the gurus and turned to a message of peace, love and LSD, its power was vastly undermined, a fact that is not well understood. While many with knowledge of the era are aware that LSD began life as a tool of the intelligence services, most believe that the drug either accidentally got out to the public, or that it was a CIA operation that backfired.

Evidence clearly indicates that the massive infusion of LSD (and other drugs as well) into the subculture was no accident. Virtually all of the acid circulating so freely in the sixties was synthesized and distributed by intelligence operatives, who were not by any stretch of the imagination 'rogue agents.'[76]

It also doesn't appear as though the drugging of the anti-war movement was an experiment that backfired. Rather, it was a well-planned operation that largely succeeded in taking the steam out of what was a potentially powerful movement, while at the

---

[75] See Martin Lee's *Acid Dreams*.

[76] See *Acid Dreams* and David Black's *Acid: The Secret History of LSD*, Vision Paperbacks, 1998. The primary financier of the clandestine LSD labs was William Mellon Hitchcock, as in Richard Mellon Scaife of the 'vast right-wing conspiracy.'

same time discrediting and marginalizing the legitimate grievances of the protestors in the eyes of more mainstream society.

The truth is that if the introduction of LSD had really backfired against the CIA, empowering the anti-war movement, the state would not have allowed the drug to remain legal and readily available throughout much of the decade. It was, after all, not until 1968 that possession of the drug was criminalized, and then only as a misdemeanor.

The truth is also that the proponents of the psychedelic movement were advising activists to drop out – to turn their backs on the system rather than fighting it. Kesey's advice to a Berkeley Vietnam Day rally, for instance, was: "Do you know how to stop the war? Just turn your backs on it, fuck it."

Leary's advice at a 'hip summit' was: "Don't vote. Don't politic. Don't petition. You can't do *anything* about America politically." Leary also claimed that "The cause of social conflict is usually neurological. The cure is biochemical," perhaps the most appalling statement made by any of the so-called leaders of the resistance movement, unless one is of the mind that the best way to deal with social conflict is to drug dissidents into a state of complacency.

The point of this rather lengthy digression is that it is quite possible for a movement to be entirely co-opted, even as outward appearances suggest otherwise, a point that should at least be considered by those in the Anarchist movement, and the Patriot movement as well.

The question remains then: where *are* we to find our fabled democracy? Perhaps we need to take another look at that much maligned concept of democratic socialism. We could begin by taking note of the fact that while it may be true that such a system has never succeeded, it is equally true that none has ever been given a fair chance.

How are we to condemn a system that has never been given a chance to succeed or fail on its own merits? And if we are so sure that such a system is inherently doomed to failure, why then have we not let them fail on their own? Why instead have we made martyrs out of men like Che Guevera, Patrice Lumumba, Salvador Allende and Jacobo Arbenz?

Why are we so afraid of this thing called socialism that we have to snuff it out immediately wherever it appears? And why do we so fear its ability to spread like a cancer to neighboring countries? Why have we always been told that if we let one domino fall, they likely all will fall?

By what force would it be possible for the 'disease' of socialism to spread? Only through the will and determination of the masses of the people could this be the case. For contrary to the disinformation fed through the far-right crowd, there is no conspiracy among the rich and powerful to institute a global socialist system.

That so many people believe that to be the case is testament to the fact that most people in this country don't really understand the meaning of the terms *fascism* and *socialism*. If they did, they would likely be able to figure out that the Rockefellers and Carnegies of the world don't really harbor a secret burning desire to nationalize their vast personal fortunes.

Their true desire is to further augment their net worth by continuing to suck the wealth out of every remaining corner of the world, under the guise of free trade. According to the belief system ingrained by the propaganda of the fascist state, 'free trade' equals freedom. It appears that all the world, then, will soon be 'free.'

Unless, that is, the American people take it upon themselves to do in the United States what the American government failed to do in Germany following World War II: denazify and decartelize the fascist state. The failure of our leaders to do so in 1945 has had tragic results for the country and for the world. Our failure as a people to do so now will have even more tragic consequences for ourselves and our children.

Appendix

World War II Casualty Estimates

Casualties:	Total	Military	Civilian
United States*	292,000	292,000	
British Commonwealth*	87,000	87,000	
United Kingdom*	357,000	297,000	60,000
	736,000	676,000	60,000
Western Front:			
Belgium*	113,000	12,000	101,000
Denmark*	4,000	2,000	2,000
France*	623,000	213,000	410,000
Netherlands*	321,000	8,000	313,000
Norway*	10,000	3,000	7,000
Finland	84,000	82,000	2,000
Italy	405,000	243,000	162,000
	1,560,000	563,000	997,000
Eastern Front:			
Bulgaria	20,000	10,000	10,000
Czechoslovakia*	315,000	10,000	305,000
Greece	475,000	90,000	385,000
Hungary	750,000	200,000	550,000
Romania	750,000	300,000	450,000
Yugoslavia*	1,550,000	300,000	1,250,000
Poland*	8,625,000	125,000	8,500,000
Germany/Austria	7,500,000	3,500,000	4,000,000
Soviet Union*	25,000,000	9,000,000	16,000,000

	44,985,000	13,535,000	31,450,000
Pacific Theater:			
Philippines*	118,000	30,000	88,000
Japan	2,100,000	1,700,000	400,000
China*	**13,500,000**	**3,500,000**	**10,000,000**
	15,718,000	5,230,000	10,488,000

*   Allied Nations

References

PART II:
Bain, Donald *The Control of Candy Jones*, Playboy Press, 1976
Balsamo, William and George Carpozi, Jr. *Crime Inc: The Inside Story of the Mafia's First 100 Years*, W.H. Allen, 1988
Blum, William *Killing Hope*, Common Courage Press, 1995
Bowart, Walter *Operation Mind Control*, Dell Publishing, 1978
Chaiken, Anton and Webster Tarpley *George Bush: An Unauthorized Biography*, www.tarpley.net/bushb.htm
Chen, Edwin "Bush Clan Poised to Become Major Political Dynasty," *Los Angeles Times*, January 20, 2001
Cockburn, Alexander and Jeffrey St. Clair *Whiteout*, Verso, 1998
Eisenberg, Dennis et.al. *Meyer Lansky: Mogul of the Mob*, Paddington Press, 1979
Gilstrap, Peter "Snatching Sinatra," *Los Angeles New Times*, May 21, 1998
Hersh, Burton *The Old Boys*, Charles Scribner's Sons, 1992
Higham, Charles *Trading With the Enemy*, Delacorte Press, 1983
Higham, Charles *American Swastika*, Doubleday, 1985
Hunt, Linda *Secret Agenda*, St. Martin's Press, 1991
Lavenda, Peter *Unholy Alliance*, Avon, 1995
Lee, Martin and Bruce Shlain *Acid Dreams*, Grove Press, 1985
Lee, Martin *The Beast Reawakens*, Routledge, 2000
Loftus, John and Mark Aarons *The Secret War Against the Jews*, St. Martin's Press, 1994
Marks, John *The Search for the Manchurian Candidate*, Times Books, 1979

McCoy, Alfred W. *The Politics of Heroin in Southeast Asia*, Harper and Row, 1972

Mosely, Leonard *Dulles*, The Dial Press, 1978

Nash, Jay Robert *Bloodletters and Bad Men, Book 3*, Warner Books, 1975

Ogden, Christopher "Pamela Harriman: Her Brilliant Career," *Time*, February 17, 1997

Risen, James "Secrets of History: The CIA in Iran," *New York Times*, April 16, 2000

Silverstein, Ken "Ford and the Fuhrer," *The Nation*, January 24, 2000

Simpson, Christopher *Blowback*, Weidenfeld and Nicholson, 1988

Simpson, Christopher *The Splendid Blond Beast*, Grove Press, 1993

Vankin, Jonathan and John Whalen *The 60 Greatest Conspiracies of All Time*, Citadel, 1996

Zepezauer, Mark *The CIA's Greatest Hits*, Odonian Press, 1994

Zezima, Michael *Saving Private Power*, Soft Skull Press, 2000

Zinn, Howard *A People's History of the United States*, Harper and Row, 1995

Encyclopaedia Britannica, www.britannica.com

The Crime Library, www.crimelibrary.com

Microsoft *Encarta* Encyclopedia

A&E Biography "Charles and Anne Lindbergh: Alone Together"

A&E Biography "J. Edgar Hoover: Personal and Confidential"

A&E Biography "Meyer Lansky: Mob Tycoon"

A&E American Justice "The Sinatra Kidnapping"

KCET "Crucible of Empire: The Spanish-American War"

KCET "The Rockefellers"

PART III:
Chapter 27:
On the Allied Bombing of Belgrade:
Tomislav Bogavac *Stanovnisto Beograda 1918-1971* (*The Population of Belgrade 1918-1971*), Muzej grada Beograda (The Museum of the City of Belgrade), 1976
Muharem Kreso *Njemacka Okupaciona Uprava U Beogradu 1941-1945* (*German Occupation Government of Belgrade 1941-1945*), Istorijski arhiv Beograda (The History Archives of Belgrade), 1979
Various authors *Beograd U Ratu I Revoluciji 1941-1945* (*Belgrade in War and Revolution 1941-1945*), Kulturni arhiv Beograda (The Culture Archives of Belgrade), 1984
Ratko Ristic *U Beogradu Rat Je Trajao 1311 Dana* (*The War Lasted 1311 Days in Belgrade*), Knjizevne novine, 1986
Background Information:
Davies, Norman *Europe*, Oxford University Press, 1996
Hersch, Burton *The Old Boys*, Charles Scribner's Sons, 1992
Higham, Charles *Trading With the Enemy*, Delacorte Press, 1983
Hunt, Linda *Secret Agenda*, St. Martin's Press, 1991
Lee, Martin *The Beast Reawakens*, Routledge, 2000
Loftus, John and Mark Aarons *The Secret War Against the Jews*, St. Martin's Press, 1994
Morris, Herman C. and Harry B. Henderson *World War II in Pictures, Volumes I and II*, Doubleday, Doran & Company, 1942
Morris, Herman C. and Harry B. Henderson *World War II in Pictures, Volume III*, The Greystone Press, 1946
Simpson, Christopher *Blowback*, Weidenfeld and Nicholson, 1988
Simpson, Christopher *The Splendid Blond Beast*, Grove Press, 1993

Zinn, Howard *A People's History of the United States*, Harper and Row, 1995
Encyclopaedia Britannica, www.britannica.com

Chapter 28:
Bowart, Walter *Operation Mind Control*, Dell Publishing, 1978
Bowart, Walter, et. al. "Mind Control Goes Public," VHS Videotape
Cockburn, Alexander and Jeffrey St. Clair "CIA Shrinks and LSD," *Counterpunch*, October 18, 1999
Delgado, Jose M.R. *Physical Control of the Mind*, Harper Colophon, 1969
Hersch, Burton *The Old Boys*, Charles Scribner's Sons, 1992
Lapon, Lenny *Mass Murderers in White Coats*, Psychiatric Genocide Research Institute, 1986
Lavenda, Peter *Unholy Alliance*, Avon, 1995
Lee, Martin and Bruce Shlain *Acid Dreams*, Grove Press, 1985
Marks, John *The Search for the Manchurian Candidate*, Times Books, 1979
Martin, Harry V. and David Caul "Mind Control," *Napa Sentinel*, August-November 1991
Schrag, Peter *Mind Control*, Pantheon, 1978
Thomas, Gordon *Journey Into Madness*, Bantam Books, 1989
Watson, Peter *War on the Mind*, Hutchinson, 1978
Encyclopaedia Britannica, www.britannica.com

Chapter 29:
Abate, Tom "Nobel Winner's Theories Raise Uproar in Berkeley," *San Francisco Chronicle*, November 13, 2000
Chaiken, Anton and Webster Tarpley *George Bush: An Unauthorized Biography*, www.tarpley.net/bushb.htm

Chase, Allan *The Legacy of Malthus: The Social Costs of the New Scientific Racism*, University of Illinois Press, 1980
Chorover, Stephan L. *From Genesis to Genocide*, MIT Press, 1983
Gaglioti, Frank "The Human Genome Project: Science, Society and Superstition," *World Socialist Web Site*, www.wsws.org
Gannon, John C. (Chairman, National Intelligence Council) "The Global Infectious Disease Threat and Its Implications for the United States," January 2000, www.cia.gov/cia/publications/nie/report/nie99-17d.html
Harris, Robert and Jeremy Paxman *A Higher Form of Killing*, Hill and Wang, 1982
Lapon, Lenny *Mass Murderers in White Coats*, Psychiatric Genocide Research Institute, 1986
Lederman, Robert "The Human Genome Project and Eugenics," *The Konformist*, www.konformist.com
Lederman, Robert "Giuliani, the Manhattan Institute, and Eugenics: The Ugly Truth Behind 'Quality of Life'," *The Konformist*, www.konformist.com
Lifton, Robert Jay *The Nazi Doctors*, Basic Books, 1986
Ogden, Christopher "Pamela Harriman: Her Brilliant Career," *Time*, February 17, 1997
Schrag, Peter *Mind Control*, Pantheon, 1978
Stannard, David E. *American Holocaust*, Oxford University Press, 1992
Thomas, Gordon *Journey Into Madness*, Bantam Books, 1989
Vankin, Jonathan and John Whalen *The 60 Greatest Conspiracies of All Time*, Citadel, 1996
Williams, Carol J. "Breeding to Further the Reich," *Los Angeles Times*, January 21, 2000
L.A. Mentary, Volume 38, Number 3, March 2000
L.A. Mentary, Volume 38, Number 10, October 2000

Encyclopaedia Britannica, www.britannica.com
A&E Biography "Charles and Anne Lindbergh: Alone Together"
The Human Genome Project Web Site, www.ornl.gov/hgmis/

Chapter 30:
Gaglioti, Frank "The Human Genome Project: Science, Society and Superstition," *World Socialist Web Site,* www.wsws.org
Gannon, John C. (Chairman, National Intelligence Council) "The Global Infectious Disease Threat and Its Implications for the United States," January 2000,
www.cia.gov/cia/publications/nie/report/nie99-17d.html
Haney, Daniel Q. "AIDS Crisis Could Turn Back Clock in Africans' Life Spans," *Los Angeles Daily News,* July 11, 2000
Maugh, Thomas H. II "AIDS to Cut Africa Life Expectancy to Under 30," *Los Angeles Times,* July 11, 2000
Maugh, Thomas H. II "UNICEF Decries Failure to Curb AIDS in Africa," *Los Angeles Times,* July 13, 2000
Nullis, Clare "AIDS Toll Expected to Worsen," *Los Angeles Daily News,* June 28, 2000
Smyth, Patrick "The Biggest Killer Among Young Black Men," *The Irish Times,* January 20, 2001

Printed in the United States
128594LV00002B/17/A

9 780595 186402